LONG-TERM CARE INSURANCE MADE SIMPLE

LES ABROMOVITZ

HEALTH INFORMATION PRESS

Los Angeles, California 90010

Library of Congress Cataloging-in-Publication Data

Abromovitz, Les.
    Long-term care insurance made simple / Les Abromovitz.
        p. cm.
    Includes index.
    ISBN 1-885987-14-5
    1. Insurance, Long-term care--United States. 2. Aged--Long-term care--
United States. I. Title.
HG9390.A27 1999
368.38'2--dc21   99-12994
                                                                      CIP

Disclaimer:
This publication is designed to offer basic and practical information on long-term care insurance. The information presented is based on the experience and interpretation of the author. Although the information has been carefully researched and checked for accuracy, currency and completeness, neither the author nor the publisher accept any responsibility or liability with regard to errors, omissions, misuse or misinterpretation.

ISBN: 1-885987-14-5

Printed in the United States of America

Health Information Press
4727 Wilshire Blvd., Suite 300
Los Angeles, CA 90010
1-800-MED-SHOP
MEDICALBOOKSTORE.COM

DEDICATION

*G*rowing old isn't so bad if there's a special person at your side. My wife, Hedy, has been that person through 25 wonderful years of marriage. Our parents have shown us that you can still be active, vibrant and fun, even as age starts to slow you down. My older sisters, Phyllis Miller and Pam Golden, and my brother-in-law, Dr. Gerald Miller, have given me hope that someday I'll be as physically fit as they are. If not, maybe they can take care of me in my old age.

ACKNOWLEDGEMENT

Editors are the caregivers of the publishing field. Maureen Lynch of Health Information Press has been extremely conscientious, dedicated, and polite in all of her dealings with me. I am grateful to her, and all of the people at Health Information Press who have guided me through this project.

TABLE OF CONTENTS

Chapter 1

PLANNING FOR
TOMORROW

My parents have a plan for staying out of a nursing home. They say that if and when the day comes when they must give up their house, they will move to an apartment or condominium. It will have to be on the first floor, since my mom hates elevators. The apartment building or condominium will need to be right next door to a McDonald's and a supermarket. My parents hope to be able to walk over for breakfast and coffee at McDonald's, enjoying the senior discount rate. For lunch and dinner, they will buy groceries and pre-prepared meals at the market.

We are keeping our fingers crossed that the plan works out for them. Although everyone knows that life does not always go as you have intended, each time we drive by a McDonald's we continue to scout the area for apartments. And when we see a group of seniors having coffee inside, we are tempted to stop and ask if they live a few doors away.

Thinking about the possibility of needing long-term care is scary. We cannot envision ourselves or a loved one in a nursing home, requiring care from others to survive. Some of us have bad memories from childhood. When we visited a grandparent or great-grandparent in a facility, known then as the "old age home," the place always smelled funny and was depressing.

Some of our memories are more recent. My wife and I recently visited her aunt who is living in a nursing home. The aunt begged for us to take her home. Then, as we left, an elderly woman with no apparent relatives grabbed my wife's hand as she passed by. She squeezed it tightly, drawing some comfort from holding someone's hand. When we left the facility, my wife cried. It was extremely painful to see her aunt at this stage in her life and to witness a perfect stranger's desperate loneliness as her life neared its end.

Most of us have heard people say that they would rather die than be in a nursing home. If and when the time comes, maybe they will feel differently. Fortunately, as this book will address in later chapters, there are many care options that can help you to avoid or at least postpone living in a nursing home.

Thankfully, all of us have choices that are a far cry from the nursing homes we grew up fearing. These choices allow many people to live out their lives with dignity and independence and to be among friends. They are able to enjoy many activities in their final days.

Because people are so different from each other, making meaningful generalizations is always problematic. We all know sixty-year-olds who act eighty, and eighty-year-olds who are as vibrant as someone half their age. Jack LaLanne, the fitness guru many of us may remember from our childhood, is still going strong in his mid-eighties. Along with an exercise regimen that would put most of us to shame, his blood pressure is 120/80. Likewise, the astronaut John Glenn, who is in his late seventies, can still withstand the rigors of space travel, while far younger people are ready to collapse after a long plane flight.

Obviously, attitude has a lot to do with it. In a letter published in the syndicated advice column "Dear Abby," a navy veteran writes to tell readers about a remarkable 93-year-old woman who lives in his residential development. The woman wakes up at 5:30 every morning and delivers newspapers at the door of all fifty homes in her neighborhood.[1]

A few years ago, an elderly Cleveland man I know told a relative that he is in the market for a new car. The man was approaching ninety and had kept his last car for over a decade. When the relative quizzed the man, asking him what features he was looking for in the vehicle, the gentleman replied without the slightest bit of hesitation that he was concerned about resale value.

This particular individual truly expected this would not be his last car purchase. Although he is no longer driving, the man is still thriving although well into his nineties. Unfortunately, there are others his age who cannot go to the bathroom themselves without the assistance of a caregiver.

Our perception of age changes as we grow older. When we are in our twenties or thirties, we think that we will have lived a long, full life by age seventy. As we grow older, however, we hope there are many more years ahead of us. As the singer/songwriter Neil Diamond wrote, life is "done too soon" for a great many people.

PLAN AHEAD

In another letter printed in "Dear Abby," a 44-year-old woman describes how exhausted she is from the constant worry, frustration, anger and guilt she feels. She, her husband and her sisters have spent a year dealing with the failing health of their parents and a grandparent. The woman writes that she wishes they would have thought ahead and planned for their declining health and abilities. Instead, all of the decisions were left up to herself, her husband and her sisters. No one is entirely happy with any of the decisions that they have made.

The letter-writer could be the poster child for the so-called "sandwich generation." She is trying to raise her own children who are ages 15 and 11, while caring for her elderly parents. The stressed-out woman is finding it difficult to juggle all of her roles. She offers some simple advice that Abby endorses, as would almost any rational person:

"I'm making sure my children won't have to go through this hell. My husband and I take excellent care of ourselves, believing prevention is one key to aging well. I plan to keep my will updated, make all my own funeral arrangements down to the last detail, select the assisted living center and/or nursing home I want to go to, and write all this down for my children. I don't want to put them in the position we've found ourselves forced into. —Any Family, Anywhere"[2]

Even if you are an extremely optimistic individual with a positive outlook who thinks and acts young, you can't go through life without planning for the day when age will catch up with you. The planning process is not a depressing act, however; it is simply preparation for a worst-case scenario. Not considering the possibility of needing assistance someday is akin to not making a will. And, just as drafting a will does not mean you are *planning* to die, preparing for old age does not bring it about faster. It simply helps to assure that your affairs will be in order just in case something does happen.

It also makes sense to consider setting up what is called a *durable power of attorney*. This document permits a representative to take care of your bills and other affairs, if that becomes necessary. A durable power of attorney authorizes a designated representative to pay expenses on your behalf.

Similarly, by signing a durable power of attorney for healthcare, your designated representative may make medical decisions on your behalf, if you become incapacitated. You may also want to make a *living will*, which would provide direction to physicians who are treating you in the final stages of life. While you can purchase forms and computer programs that will help you to prepare these documents yourself, it is probably best to consult with an attorney who specializes in elder law.

As distasteful as it is to consider the possibility of death or incapacity, to not prepare for what may happen is to bury your head in the sand. Most of us guard against events we hope never occur. We buy life insurance, even though we are young. We purchase health insurance, even though we are healthier than we have ever been. Even if we are working, we put money aside in case we lose our job. It is all part of being an adult and recognizing that certain events are beyond our control.

"Living life to its fullest" isn't inconsistent with planning for the inevitability of death or the possibility that you may need long-term care at some point. It is possible to plan ahead without losing a positive attitude toward your future.

RISK MANAGEMENT

Every family should engage in risk management, which is just what corporations do. Large companies appoint a risk manager to look at the potential hazards that may be encountered and to take the appropriate steps to guard against their occurrence. These risk managers analyze the hazards a company faces. To guard against these pitfalls, the risk manager may buy insurance to protect the company. The risk manager, however, does much more for a company than just buy insurance. Sometimes the corporation decides to "self-insure" against potential losses. It does this by putting aside funds to cover any contingencies that may occur. The risk manager is also on the lookout for ways to prevent accidents from occurring. The person in that position implements loss prevention programs and seeks to minimize the adverse effects of an accident, should one occur.

Many people act in the same fashion as risk managers, without even knowing it. They adopt a lifestyle that will enable them to extend their lives and remain healthier for a longer period. Unfortunately, there is no way to prevent old age from occurring. Furthermore, certain accidents, diseases or other tragedies may befall us no matter how many steps we take to prevent them. While you can be the quintessential risk manager for your family, you may still run into unavoidable problems.

MINIMIZING YOUR NEED FOR LONG-TERM CARE

There are ways, however, to minimize the risk of needing long-term care —or at least to delay the point in time when you will need it. A healthy lifestyle is a good starting point, and a positive attitude also makes a big difference. Another very important step is finding a living arrangement where you can fend for yourself for as long as possible (by the way, that living arrangement does not necessarily need to be next door to a McDonald's!).

Seriously, just as you must child-proof a home when your children are young, steps must be taken to deal with aging. You can install an elevated toilet seat or grab bars in the bathroom. If you are becoming forgetful, there are automatic stove turnoff devices that shut off the oven after a certain amount of time. To avoid falls, you can get rid of throw rugs or secure them to the floor. You can even hire senior care consultants who come to your home to perform safety analyses and offer suggestions.

There are even specific ways to redecorate and remodel your home with an eye toward your sunset years. *Elder Design: Designing and Furnishing a Home for Your Later Years* (Penguin, 1997), is just one book of many available that offers tips on altering your house to accommodate the effects of aging. Rosemary Bakker, the author, suggests specific colors that compensate for reduced vision and provides tips on bump-free furniture arrangement.

In addition to allowing you to stay in your home for years longer, certain home improvements may help reduce your taxes. Installing a wheelchair ramp or some other improvement for medical purposes may be tax-deductible. The cost, in certain instances, is viewed as a medical expense. Remember, however, that medical expenses must be more than 7.5 percent of your adjusted gross income before the deduction does you any good.

You may need to do more than just make changes in your existing house. As they get on in years, a great many people move out of the two-story family home that holds so many memories. In general, most older people are tired of going upstairs to get to certain rooms. Some are willing to buy a two-story house, but only if the master bedroom is on the first floor and they can put their grandchildren in the upstairs bedroom when the kids come for a visit.

Many in the elderly population prefer to scale down to smaller, one-story homes, whether it be a ranch-style home or a condominium. Sometimes the house may be in a residential development where the maintenance is taken care of by the community in exchange for a fee. Most older people will shy away from the second floor in a two-story condominium if it has no elevator. Even if they do not have problems with the steps initially, these individuals realize that it may become an issue for them at some point. At one condominium development, residents on the second floor realized they had not planned ahead for their aging bodies. They sought to add an elevator to service the second floor units, much to the chagrin of the first floor residents who did not want to share in this expense.

A news-feature television show ran a story in 1998 about an 80-year-old woman in Pembroke Pines, Florida, who bought a "home of the future" from a well-known construction company. The home contained an electronic device, which she called Leonardo, that was supposed to do things such as turn on the lights for her and even make emergency phone calls. Unfortunately, the device tended to ignore her commands and sometimes flipped the switches on the wrong appliances. Nevertheless, this technology may soon be perfected, and someday automated assistance will be available at the sound of your voice.

Even if you are a positive-thinking, active and healthy individual who hopes to live a long, full life, you must face the risk of needing long-term care. That does not necessarily mean you should buy a long-term care policy. It simply means you should strive for a lifestyle that will let you remain independent for as long as possible. Maybe that risk management strategy will mean staying in your own house but bringing in household help when it becomes necessary, or adding a chair walker to take you to the second floor. Even though you can take care of your lawn now, you will want to budget for the day when it becomes necessary to hire someone. Or maybe you will decide to find a living arrangement now that will meet your needs for the long term.

Just as attitude differs from one person to the next, so do preferences, making it hard to find a solution that will satisfy everybody. One elderly man, for example, refuses to give up cutting the grass even though it is clear the yard is too big for him. Furthermore, he will not hire someone to cut the grass, because no one can do it well enough to please him. Also, he will not move into an apartment because he values his privacy. Nevertheless, keeping the house maintained in accordance with his high standards is impossible. He has placed himself in a difficult situation.

Similarly, an older woman who lives in a fully maintained community cannot keep her home clean any longer. Although she can afford household help, the woman cannot stand the thought of a stranger in her house. She is afraid that the person will steal from her or may take advantage of her in some other way.

While there are options that could keep people like these two out of a long-term care facility for the indefinite future, they unfortunately cannnot or will not accept these solutions. Chapter 17 discusses how geriatric care managers are able to deal with these kinds of problems.

OPTIONS FOR INDEPENDENT LIVING

As our society ages, it is changing to allow older people more options so they can live independently. For example, many utility companies have a service where a third person is notified if an elderly individual fails to pay a bill. Many businesses offer automatic payment plans, so that charges are automatically deducted from the individual's account. This also means that the individual, young or old, is relieved from some of the day-to-day paperwork. Even Social Security offers direct deposit to ensure that checks are not lost and that older citizens do not need to run to the bank each month. In the same way, some companies have made provisions so that pension checks may be deposited directly into a bank account.

Along with social service programs such as "Meals on Wheels" which bring food to the elderly, there are also businesses that will deliver meals to the elderly or shut-ins. While this may seem expensive, for someone who cannot leave the house without assistance, it will still be less costly than most assisted living situations.

Some condominium communities offer shuttle buses to the local super-market. If this is not available, there may be a neighbor who wants to make a few extra dollars by picking up groceries for those who are unable to leave their homes. Arrangements such as these may make it possible for you or a loved one to live independently for a longer period. Of course, it does not solve all the problems of those who are losing the ability to live on their own.

In the community where I grew up, a neighbor had her mother living downstairs. Her living area was self-contained and the situation worked well for many years. Unfortunately, the elderly mother cooked while the rest of the family was away. On too many occasions, she forgot about pots she had left on the stove with the burners on. Eventually, the family had to find a personal care residence for her to live.

More recently, a husband attempted to care for his wife who was wheelchair-bound. Every night, a neighbor would help him to lift and bathe her. It was hard work but he wanted his wife to stay with him at home for as long as possible. Eventually the neighbor who assisted the couple moved away. The man reluctantly found a different living arrangement for his wife.

Practicing risk management may not mean you will completely avoid needing long-term care, but it can help you to live independently and stay in familiar surroundings for as long as possible. In offering advice on whether long-term care insurance is worthwhile for you, this book operates from the premise that most people want to live independently for as long as they possibly can. It also assumes that living with one's child is not an option for the person in need of long-term care.

Another assumption is that those who can no longer live independently still want and deserve the best care available to help them live out their days. No matter how old they are or what situation they find themselves in, people receiving long-term care should be treated with dignity and respect. Even if they do not have family members who visit them, there should be a caring staff that sees to their needs.

Key Points: The Short Course on Long-Term Care Insurance

- *You cannot stop the effects of aging, but you or a loved one can prepare for the day when long-term care becomes necessary. If you take steps now, you may be able to stay in your house for a lot longer.*

- *As distasteful as it is to consider, it is wise to start thinking about ways for you or a loved one to remain independent for as long as possible. This may mean moving to a smaller house, condominium or apartment. You should also start thinking about bringing in help to meet your personal needs as you age or to assist a loved one. Consider this activity as a form of risk management, such as is practiced by corporations to identify and guard against potential problems.*

- *Talk to a lawyer who specializes in elder law. Every adult needs a will that advises how to distribute their property in the event of death. You may also wish to have a living will, a durable power of attorney that addresses your finances, and a durable power of attorney for health-care decisions.*

Chapter 2

HOUSING OPTIONS FOR THE AGING

When I was the associate producer of a program on public television several years ago, part of my job was to survey people on the street and find out what questions they had regarding long-term care insurance or other topics. One day on Las Olas Boulevard, one of Fort Lauderdale's well-known tourist spots, a woman in her early twenties had a question that fit into the topic for discussion. Perhaps she was ready to ask anything to be on camera, but the crux of her question was this: "My grandfather is retiring, so we need to find a place for him to live. How do we find the right retirement home?"

Maybe we were not communicating effectively, but it certainly sounded as if the young woman felt her grandfather's life was over. He was retired, and so now it was time to put him in a home. Time for grandpa to be "put out to pasture."

Usually, however, retirement does not mean it is time to move from your house into a retirement community. *The New York Times* recently wrote about a condominium called Kings Point in Delray Beach, Florida. Over twenty years ago, seniors purchased units and today they are still living there. Additional units are now being purchased by seniors who are decades younger. Two generations of older Americans are living there.[1]

The point is, you cannot pigeon-hole the aging population. Many are extremely active and engage in more activities than people half of their age. Some ninety-year-olds are capable of living independently, while a few younger retirees need some kind of assistance. Because of these differences, no single retirement housing arrangement is right for everyone.

West of Boca Raton, Florida, in one community, a woman turning 90 years old threw herself a party in the clubhouse of her condominium. It would have been a wonderful affair, except that the condominium rules prohibited anyone under 18 from entering the clubhouse. As a result, the woman's two great-grandchildren could not come to the party. The children, age 7 and 5, had to stay in her apartment with their mother.

The administrator explained that the condo could not make an exception for the 90-year-old woman's birthday party. After all, rules are rules, and they must be universally enforced. Otherwise, she said, people would be in her office the next day, demanding to know why an exception had been made.

Whether you are young or old, there may be restrictions that you cannot tolerate. Your friends may not be able to use the recreational facilities; or you cannot use the pool between certain hours. Some developments don't permit the posting of "for sale" signs, which makes the community nice to look at, but which makes it very difficult when the time comes to sell your house.

Unfortunately, this is the way life is in many condominium communities. The "condo sheriffs" or "condo commandos," as they are called, seem to do nothing else except look for violations of the community's many rules. They are quick to point out infringements, unless enforcement of the rules would adversely affect them.

Yet other communities lack any rules and a "sheriff" to enforce them. A condominium law advisor who writes a column for a newspaper and answers readers' questions described a situation where one third-floor condo dweller let his dog do its business on his porch, and then swept it onto the common area below. In other communities, dog owners are told to get rid of their pets, because the animals are a pound or two over the weight limit.

In some communities, wars between neighbors erupt on a daily basis. Mailboxes are filled with poison pen letters from disgruntled homeowners. The president of the homeowners' association pleads for board members to stop maligning each other. The president himself is accused of fraud and dishonesty in the purchase of two water coolers for the clubhouse.

If you have watched any of the episodes of the television sitcom "Seinfeld" where Jerry Seinfeld visits his parents who live in South Florida, you probably have seen a negative view of condominium living. In one episode, Jerry's dad is accused of stealing money from the condominium association because residents see him driving around in a Cadillac that Jerry purchased for him. The most damning evidence of the theft comes when the Seinfelds are seen paying regular prices for dinner, instead of taking advantage of the "early bird special." In another episode, the condominium development is in an uproar because Jerry accepts a pen as a gift from a friend of his father's.

While "Seinfeld" derives its humor from exaggerating everyday problems, there may be real-life evidence that fewer people want to move to retirement communities in traditional areas. In the November 14, 1997 issue of *The Wall Street Journal,* June Fletcher wrote that a new generation of older Americans, "see the traditional retirement spots as dull and socially isolating." According to the article, they are returning to the "Snow Belt" to retire. Taking note of this trend, developers of retirement communities like the Del Webb Corp., see a market for huge retirement communities in places other than traditional retirement spots such as Florida or Arizona.[2]

A company spokesperson for Del Webb observed that people want to remain near their workplaces. Many want to work part-time or to continue on as consultants for their former employer. Furthermore, they want to maintain relationships with colleagues.

Experts quoted in the *Wall Street Journal* article said they expect baby boomers will make several moves after retiring. First, they will move from their big home, where they raised their family. Next they will to a resort in a warmer climate, if only for part of the year. The third and potentially final move will be to live with or to be near children and grandchildren.

This new generation of older Americans is more active and affluent than its predecessors. To satisfy this market, Del Webb is building a huge golfing community northwest of Chicago. Along with golf, the community will offer tennis, swimming, bridge and aerobics. It will have fiber-optic cable to satisfy the computer users in the development. And, of course, snow removal is part of the package, because even active older people are not necessarily inclined to continue that back-breaking activity.

Senior housing construction is booming, and not just in Florida. According to a survey of developers of housing for the over-seventy age group, Texas has the most units under construction. The rest of the top ten are Florida, California, Arizona, North Carolina, Georgia, South Carolina, Connecticut, New Jersey and Pennsylvania.

No matter where they live, most people would like to remain active and independent as they grow older. College towns are considered to be hot spots for retirement. Many retirees like having a university close by so they can take advantage of educational offerings, teach or volunteer.[3]

In Northfield, Minnesota, the Cannon Valley Elder Collegium holds classes for a different type of student. Most students are over 65 year old—and many are in their eighties. The classes are taught by a group of retired professors and academics. They are reasonably-priced and last about eight weeks. The author Jon Jeter, a writer for *The Washington Post,* joked that financial aid is more likely to come in the form of a pension than a parent or Pell grant.[4]

CHOICES, CHOICES AND MORE CHOICES

A lot of people talk a great deal about what they will do when they get older. According to them, they will move to a retirement community, or scale back. But while many of them talk about that day, few really take steps in that direction.

When we were scouting the market for a house, my wife and I looked at one home that was owned by a couple in their seventies. They were Florida residents, but talked about moving near their children in California. At the time, the husband could barely get out of his chair without assistance. To make matters worse, the house was overflowing with every possession they ever bought in their lifetime, as well as every gift and souvenir. Because they looked so old and their health seemed to be failing, we feared that the couple would not live through the move.

Later, the real estate agent told us that their home had been on and off the market for years. The couple was unable to deal with people coming through their home. When a potential buyer was about to make an offer, the couple got cold feet. Last we checked, they still had not moved.

Moving is difficult, no matter what age you are. Furthermore, as your health fails it becomes increasingly difficult to uproot yourself and deal with the turmoil that goes hand-in-hand with moving. Nevertheless, in South Florida, we see many elderly residents who are relocating to larger, single-family homes in guarded and gated communities.

The growing older population has a great many choices of where to live. There are even communities that require residents to be older than age 55 or some other specified age. You are not allowed to sell your unit to someone who is under 55. Generally, these communities do not provide any type of long-term care.

Yet even though they are getting on in years, many people do not want to live in communities that are strictly for older adults. They like seeing young people and do not mind having children in the neighborhood. There are plenty of communities that have a nice mixture of young and old people. According to the Joint Center for Housing Studies at Harvard University, only about nine percent of the over-seventy population lives in age-restricted housing. Pamela Reeves, a real estate columnist for the Scripps Howard News Service, writes that six percent of that group lives in age-restricted housing that offers no long-term care services.[5]

The New York State Office for the Aging identifies numerous housing alternatives on its internet site (*http://www.aging.state.ny.us/nysofa/home.htm*). Some of these housing options have been developed by public organizations, and others by private organizations. Some are subsidized by the government. There are housing alternatives that provide for a number of services such as meals, transportation, housekeeping, security, personal care, and nursing care. The Office for the Aging wisely points out that even if services are not provided, residents may purchase them separately or seek assistance from a community agency.

The New York Office for the Aging also notes these housing alternatives go by different names and do not always offer the same services. Categories of housing often overlap. Some of the categories are:

- Senior Housing Developments
- Naturally Occurring Retirement Communities
- Congregate Housing Developments
- Shared Housing Alternatives
- Enriched Housing Program
- Family Type Homes
- Adult Homes
- Assisted Living Programs.

California has thousands of residential care homes. They are also known as "board and care homes," and provide non-medical, custodial care. Most of these residential care homes have six or fewer residents. Generally, larger insitutions are called assisted living facilities.

Residential care homes are not permitted to offer skilled nursing services. They can, however, provide assistance with the activities of daily living, otherwise known as ADLs.

Residential care is usually far less expensive than a nursing home. The cost will depend upon the size of the residential care home and the area where it is located. A private apartment will cost much more than a studio or shared living space. Prices range from a low of $700 to thousands of dollars per month.

The person living in a residential care setting can still carry on a "normal" life. Residents conduct their usual activities, but have access to the assistance of others.

INDEPENDENT LIVING VERSUS ASSISTED LIVING

Categorizing housing options is much like classifying mutual funds. Like mutual funds, there are many hybrids that do not distinctly fall into one particular category.

Two broad categories are *independent living* versus *assisted living*. As the name suggests, assisted living is for individuals who need assistance with day-to-day activities. It is much more than just personal care. Assisted living is a middle ground between independent living and a nursing home. Assisted living facilities are a residential alternative for those who require some amount of care. According to AARP in Washington, DC, the fastest growing housing option is assisted living residences.[6] Assisted living is a happy medium between one's own home and a full nursing facility.

One community may offer both independent living and assisted living options. For instance, some senior rental communities advertise that they are for older adults, but that assisted living is available, if needed. In these cases, the cost of assisted living services will be added on to the price already being paid. Typically, assisted living residents pay a monthly rental fee and are charged separately for additional services that become necessary.

Whereas some retirement communities offer assisted living as an additional service, many facilities are exclusively for assisted living. All of their residents are people who cannot function totally independently.

Assisted living may not mean the same thing at different retirement communities. In addition, assisted living residences are often described by various names, including: residential care homes, adult congregate living, congregate senior housing, community-based residential facilities, board and care homes, adult care homes, and domiciliary care facilities.

Alzheimer's units are frequently found within assisted living facilities and specialize in the care of people with Alzheimer's disease. Not all assisted living facilities provide care for Alzheimer's patients. Frequently, assisted living programs will limit the types of services offered.

The marvelous thing about assisted living is that it can help someone avoid confinement to a nursing home. In an assisted living situation, the person will probably have a higher quality of life at less cost than he would pay at a nursing home. Assisted living residences combine several levels of care in a residential, rather than an institutional setting.

LIFE CARE AND CONTINUING CARE COMMUNITIES

The setting in the Mary Higgins Clark popular thriller, *Moonlight Becomes You*, is an expensive retirement home called Latham Manor. This retirement home has a unit that is set aside for long-term nursing care. Admission fees start at $200,000 for a large private room and bath, while a two-bedroom suite is $500,000. Residents also pay a monthly maintenance fee of $2000.

In exchange for these fees, the residents receive full and exclusive use of the agreed-upon apartment during his or her lifetime. At death, ownership reverts to the residence. The apartment is then available to be sold again. In this novel, guests at the elegant retirement home begin dying, which leaves their apartment suspiciously available for resale.

You will have to read the book to find out the rest of the plot. Needless to say, the author does a much better job of telling the story than I do! While the book is, of course, fiction, it does point out some of the pitfalls associated with buying into a life care community. That is, you might die before getting to enjoy it for too long.

Assuming *Moonlight Becomes You* does not scare you off, life care and continuing care communities are attractive in many ways. They offer many housing options from independent living facilities to skilled nursing care. Residents move from one setting to another, depending upon the level of care that is needed. Nevertheless, they stay within the community, so they are still in familiar surroundings.

Some of these communities have medical personnel on-site, whereas others offer transportation to physicians and other services. Many require an up-front payment as well as monthly fees. Recently, some communities began offering their services on a rental basis and health care coverage is paid for when needed.

California distinguishes between a *continuing care community* and a *life care community*. A true life care community must:

- Guarantee health care coverage for life without exception;
- Guarantee that residents will not lose their residence, even if their financial resources are exhausted;
- Have a nursing facility within the community; and
- Guarantee that the particular unit selected when the contract is signed will not be taken for any reason.

Because of these strict requirements, few continuing care communities in California can bill themselves as a life care community.

Most life care communities ask for a significant amount of money up front which is not always refundable. The traditional arrangement is to make a life care endowment which will cover the resident's care throughout his or her lifetime. In California, the entrance fees range from $10,000 to $500,000, and monthly fees range from $600 to well over $2,000.

According to the California Registry's Online Senior Housing & Senior Care Database (*http://www.calregistry.com*), the goal of continuing care and life care communities is to allow residents to "age in place." Residents will be able to receive the full continuum of care as they age. The only exception is when residents must be hospitalized.

Continuing care and life care communities might serve as a substitute for long-term care insurance. By paying the entrance fee, the buyer purchases protection against the risk of needing long-term care. Continuing care communities offer independent living, as well as skilled nursing care. Living in a continuing care or life care community can reduce the risk that you will need to leave your home to get long-term care.

The National Association of Insurance Commissioners (NAIC) reports that some continuing care communities offer or require you to buy long-term care insurance. Sometimes, the policies are sponsored by the continuing care community. An insurance company writes the policy. To qualify, you must be a resident or on a waiting list for the continuing care community. You must also meet the insurance company's medical eligibility requirements.

Continuing care and life care communities can be very expensive. It is imperative that any contract you sign be reviewed carefully. The contract will stipulate how much nursing care is provided for the initial fee. The contract will also spell out your losses, if you decide to move or if you die. Communities have different refund policies, but usually you will lose a small percentage of your entrance fee even if you leave within a short amount of time.

There are other points to remember before selecting a continuing care or life care community for yourself or a loved one, including:

- Get a lawyer to look over the paperwork. Make sure that all verbal assurances are put in writing.
- Find out if the facility has insurance that protects you if it experiences financial difficulties.
- Call the regulators in your state and see if they have inspected the facility, examining them for both financial and health code violations.
- Make certain that the facility has been in business for a lengthy period. Find out if the management has been stable.
- Talk to the residents to gauge how satisfied they are. Try to speak with them when the staff is not around.
- Discuss the decision you are about to make with family members and friends.
- Ask about any restrictions that may cause a problem for you, like conditions on when children or grandchildren are permitted to visit.

Remember, the decision you make can affect how you or a loved one spend the rest of your life. It should not be made hastily.

ADVERTISEMENTS FOR RETIREMENT HOUSING

The advertisements for retirement housing provide a sense of what living arrangements people want as they grow older —or at least what the marketers perceive they want. They reveal a great deal about the housing options and services that are available and how much they cost. The ads can help you to decide if a particular situation is right for you, or your parent, spouse or relative. In later chapters, we'll look at whether long-term care insurance will cover the care and services provided by these facilities.

Religion is very important to some people. Some residences advertise their religious-affiliation and promote the fact that a chapel or synagogue is on the premises. Other facilities make it clear that they have no religious affiliation.

One common theme in ads promoting retirement housing is that "the best is yet to come." One ad encourages potential residents to make the most of their life and to live where they can enjoy "a social calendar brimming with cultural and educational activities." Another advertisement encourages readers to live life to its fullest.

The ads promise that life there will be akin to living at a resort and that retirement will be a full time vacation. In fact, the same companies that we associate with hotels and resorts —e.g., Marriott and Hyatt— are now involved in building assisted living residences. An assisted living rental community says it offers the ambiance of a fine hotel. The inference you are encouraged to make is that you are not moving into an assisted living residence, you are going on vacation.

One assisted living facility even offers a nightly turndown service. If the staff were to leave a mint on the pillow and tiny bottles of shampoo in the bathroom, residents may feel as if they are staying at the Ritz-Carlton! Another continuing care community carries this theme further, when it describes itself as "the retirement resort with continuing care."

Most ads seem to be targeted toward aging individuals who want to remain active, not spend the rest of their days in a rocking chair. One ad points out that the residence is close to local arts and cultural organizations. At another life care community, the residents can enjoy golf, tennis, croquet, and a world class spa. The clubhouse contains a theater, library, computer center, card rooms, arts and crafts studio, cocktail lounge and billiards room. An ad for a different life care community depicts two older gentlemen canoeing.

The advertisements do, however, recognize that some people have a more sedentary existence in mind. One states, "You can be as active or relaxed as you wish in our carefree surroundings." It is apparent that being carefree is another common theme. Ads emphasize that residents will have peace of mind with no worries or responsibilities.

Other ads carry that theme further. An assisted living residence promises worry-free, independent living with a safety net of personal care. The facility offers 24-hour professional assistance to give a helping hand, if necessary. A different assisted living residence advertises that you will have an emergency pull cord, linking you to management personnel 24 hours a day. A Marriott assisted living residence says it combines the privacy of living in your own home with the security of knowing a caring professional staff is nearby.

Similar themes run through the ads directed at the children seeking the right living arrangement for a parent. These ads promise children that they will have the peace of mind that comes with knowing their parents are in good hands. One ad asks, "Do you know if your mother remembered to have lunch today?" Other ads assure them that their parents will get the right food, will get to their doctor and will enjoy the company of friends.

Ads directed at children play upon the children's guilt, concern, obligation and responsibility. Most children want to feel that an aging parent is safe, well-cared for and secure. A residential community for people with Alzheimer's disease advertises that it offers family "coping" groups. Another assisted living facility features a special care unit for the memory impaired. The unit provides care for individuals who are confused, agitated, unable to communicate, and suffering from memory loss.

The ads assure readers that the resident will be treated like family. Employees are described as enthusiastic, highly-trained, and dedicated. One residence advertises that its employees are selected for their warm and compassionate nature. Another ad describes its employees as "caring professionals who love what they do." "Caring is a lot more than a job," states one ad. Another residence's slogan is, "Where caring is from the heart."

Most of the ads assure potential residents that they can provide more care, if it is needed. Many communities offer independent living, but have an assisted living residence on the premises if necessary. Rehabilitative and home health care services are available. There may be a special facility on the grounds for residents with Alzheimer's disease or memory disorders. The theme seems to be that you will be taken care of, even if your health deteriorates. Other ads, however, emphasize that health and wellness programs are offered to keep the resident's health from deteriorating.

Price is usually not mentioned in these ads. A Hyatt assisted living facility stresses that it is "the perfect blend of quality, style, service and value." A Marriott ad highlights that residents only pay for the level of service and care they require. The ad declares, "Yes, the Marriott name adds value to Assisted Living. But value doesn't mean it costs more." A different Marriott advertisement promises three months free rent. Marriott even offers a $500 referral fee at some facilities, if the person referred moves in.

A rental retirement community advertises that it offers an "affordable annual lease." An ad for "active senior apartment homes" offers monthly rents as low as $519. Transportation is available, as well as a noon meal. The odds are good that these services involve an additional fee. A senior living residence is not far behind, with a charge of only $995 per month.

At one assisted living facility, the monthly charge is $895 per month, which is certainly a bargain if true. Not far behind is a rental retirement community, offering independent and assisted living, from $1,295.

While assisted living offers a cheaper alternative to nursing homes, the operative word in ads like this is "from." In Pittsburgh, an assisted living residence for seven seniors runs from $1,190 to $1,690 per month. A larger facility in South Florida offers assisted living residences starting at $1,195 per month. A Marriott assisted living residence in Fort Lauderdale advertises private units ranging from $1,675 to $2,100 per month. Shared units are $1,300 to $1,475 per month. Included in these fees are three meals per day, laundry services, housekeeping, and cable.

A premier life care resort community advertises entrances fees from $155,000 and monthly fees from $1,495. Another life care community promises that your monthly rate will not change as a result of your need for a higher level of care, including assisted living or skilled nursing. Obviously, however, the monthly rate may increase for other reasons.

A common theme of almost every ad is that you will not be neglected or forgotten. One residence says it offers "care that doesn't sacrifice your dignity or your lifestyle." Communities are described as vibrant, luxurious, cheerful, sunny, spacious, private, charming, and homey. Another states that residents love "the beautiful settings that look just like first-class resorts, but feel just like home." In a different ad, the grounds are described as lush and park-like. A Charlotte, North Carolina continuing care retirement community describes its grounds as a campus with well-appointed apartments and beautiful cottages.

The images created connote freedom, as well as independence. Few older people want to find themselves trapped in a semi-private room, unable to leave at will. Even if you are unable to get out much without assistance, a view of the grounds is important too. Residences advertise that you overlook beautifully landscaped courtyards or tropical foliage. Another emphasizes that it is built in a dramatic setting, surrounding a beautiful man-made lake which has a picturesque gazebo in the middle of it.

In fact, most ads appeal to our desire to remain as independent as possible, even as our health deteriorates because of aging or some other cause. An assisted living rental community advertises that it "offers security without sacrificing independence." Other residences promise that the choice is yours as to what activities you will participate in during the course of a day.

Ideally, these communities live up to their advertising and meet all of the needs of their residents. If they even come close and provide comfort, as well as care for their residents, they are worth every dime. Throughout this book, as we discuss long-term care insurance, the ultimate goal is staying independent for as long as possible and obtaining the best care available if it becomes necessary. Even as you or a loved one becomes reliant on others to provide long-term care, the best case scenario is that the care is provided by compassionate people who treat the individual with dignity.

Key Points: The Short Course on Long-Term Care Insurance

- *There are housing options that are less expensive than a nursing home and far less restrictive. The resident can enjoy privacy, plus supportive services. Assisted living offers a middle ground between totally independent living and a nursing home.*

- *Buying into a life care community may minimize your need for long-term care insurance. Unfortunately, these communities are usually too expensive for people with modest incomes.*

- *Subsidized senior housing can be a less expensive alternative for individuals with low to moderate incomes. Some of these facilities offer assistance to residents, even though they live independently in apartments.*

- *Don't rely upon advertisements to select the best living arrangement for you or a loved one who may need long-term care down the road. Talk to the residents when they are able to speak freely. Check with state agencies that regulate these facilities to determine if they have records on complaints filed against them or the results of inspections of the facilities.*

- *Always ask about extra fees and charges. The "from" price being advertised will usually not include all of the services described in the marketing materials.*

Chapter 3

WHAT IS LONG-TERM CARE?

I have a friend who has a summer home on an island in Buzzard's Bay, near Boston. When he is down in Florida, a neighbor who is in his eighties takes care of his lawn up north, as well as the yards of several other island residents. By cutting lawns, the octogenarian supplements his pension. Age has taken its toll, however. While he can still cut lawns with his riding mower, the man had to give up digging for clams, and sticks to fishing. Similarly, many other residents of the island are still going strong, even though they are in their eighties. Two elderly sisters can be seen every morning, power walking through town.

My wife's great-grandfather enjoyed good health into his nineties. We were never quite sure whether it was his work as a caretaker for a cemetery or the shot of Old Granddad that he drank every day. Even after he had a stroke and was unable to speak, the twinkle remained in his eye. When anyone asked how he felt, the elderly gentleman would gesture that he felt with his fingers, a joke he still enjoyed after decades of using it. Despite his stroke, my wife's great-grandfather was able to stay at home until his death. His children lived in the house and took care of him.

While we all hope that we, too, will be cutting lawns, power walking, or taking care of a cemetery in our old age, there is a distinct possibility that someone will be taking care of us. Long-term care refers to the assistance that may become necessary when you are unable to care for yourself. While it may be needed simply because of the effects of aging, care of this kind can also be required due to an accident or illness.

Long-term care differs from acute care. Acute care refers to treatment of a certain illness or condition over a short period of time. Someone with an acute condition is medically unstable and requires frequent monitoring by medical professionals.

THE "SANDWICH GENERATION"

Recently, while waiting for a late-evening flight, I observed a middle-age man tending to his disabled father. During the long wait, the man helped his father go to the bathroom and brought dinner to him. The man cut his dad's food and saw to it that his father ate and was comfortable during delay after delay. When I last saw the men, it was 3:30 in the morning and the son was attempting to find a wheelchair for his father. Exasperated by an airline employee who did not want to part with a wheelchair, the son complained for the first time about needing to be at work in four hours.

Whether it is in the air or on the ground, caregiving takes an infinite amount of patience. Although long-term care is commonly perceived as a stay in a nursing home, it also refers to help at home with activities such as cooking, bathing, getting dressed or household chores. Most often, long-term care is provided at home by friends and relatives. Providing this care can be an enormous psychological and financial hardship. Caregivers may find that they have little or no time for themselves or their own family.

The so-called "sandwich generation" has the responsibility of caring for aging parents, while at the same time they raise their own children. According to the popular psychologist Dr. Joyce Brothers, baby boomers can expect to become the most "sandwiched" in history. A married couple is likely to spend more years caring for an elderly parent than raising their own child. [1]

If you work hard, you are undoubtedly exhausted at the end of the day. You drag yourself home, almost too tired to cook dinner. If you add children to the mix, your day only begins when you get home from work. There seems to be no end to your responsibilities. But just imagine adding the care of an elderly parent to your duties. Whether that parent lives with you or across town, there are not enough hours in the day to handle all of your obligations.

Dr. Brothers notes that seven million people in the United States are acting as unpaid caregivers. Seventy-five percent of them are women. A report from the National Family Caregivers Association shows that intense caregivers suffer from depression and back pain, along with financial stress.

It is no wonder that members of the "sandwich generation" feel pulled in all directions. They have too many responsibilities to deal with and too many needs to satisfy. It is sometimes impossible for them to add care of their elderly parents to a plate that is already overflowing.

OPTIONS FOR THOSE IN NEED OF LONG-TERM CARE

Nursing homes are just one option for those in need of long-term care. Other alternatives may include at-home care or a community-based pro-gram. Care at home allows the person to remain in familiar surroundings and be more independent. Institutional care is often a last resort and may be necessary only if the individual needs constant attention.

Long-term care encompasses a wide range of nursing, medical and social services. As the term implies, the care is required over an extended period. It is not just the elderly who need it. There are too many instances where a young person requires long-term care because of an accident or medical condition. In addition, Alzheimer's disease, strokes and other problems befall many who are not "elderly" by any definition.

The government's Health Care Financing Administration has sug-gested many alternatives to nursing home care, such as:

- Home Health Care
- Respite Care
- Adult Day Care Centers
- Foster Care
- Residential Care in a Board and Care Home
- Retirement Communities
- Hospice Care.

Respite care is designed to give the primary caregiver a well-deserved rest. When the primary caregiver needs a break from the day-to-day strain of providing long-term care, these services can be utilized. Respite care is provided by nursing homes and assisted living faciliites for a fee. There are also alternative caregivers who provide respite care on an informal basis.

Adult day care centers have become increasingly popular. Many are run by non-profit agencies and the cost is sometimes based upon ability to pay. Adult day care centers run on the same principles as day care for children. They are open during customary business hours, so caregivers can go to work during the day and administer long-term care themselves during evenings and weekends.

Foster care is much like services offered in a foster home. The person in need of long-term care lives with someone who can help with the activities of daily living. Sometimes the person in need of care pays for these services. In other instances, a government program will pay for foster care.

Usually, *board and care homes* are small, private residential facilities. Residents receive all meals, as well as personal care. These homes are not for individuals who need the high level of care available in a nursing home.

In the context of long-term care, some *retirement communities* offer much more than shuffleboard and canasta. As was mentioned in Chapter 2, life care and continuing care communities offer many housing options, from independent living facilities to skilled nursing care. Many require an up-front payment, as well as monthly fees. Some have on-site medical personnel and provide transportation to physicians and other services.

Hospice care provides support for the dying and their families. Some hospice programs let patients stay in their homes or create a home-like atmosphere in a special institution. Usually, hospice patients have a life expectancy of six months or less. The hospice worker helps the family cope with the emotional upheaval caused by the grave situation.

LEVELS OF CARE

Many services offered to the patient and the caregiver fall under the heading of long-term care. Long-term care insurance policies do not always distinguish between levels of care, nor do they all classify the care in a particular category. Nevertheless, it is helpful to distinguish between levels of care and settings of care.

Skilled Nursing Care

Skilled nursing care (SNC) is the highest level of care. Skilled nursing care can only be performed by or under the supervision of skilled medical personnel. The care must be provided pursuant to a doctor's orders; that is, the nurses or therapists must be following a treatment plan. Sometimes, the skilled nursing care is performed in the person's home. It is available twenty-four hours a day. A skilled nursing facility is an alternative to hospitalization for some acute medical conditions.

Medicare does not pay for around-the-clock skilled nursing care in your home. For Medicare reimbursement, the skilled nursing care must be performed in a skilled nursing facility. The long-term care insurer may not have this requirement. The long-term care policy will generally view skilled nursing care as care given by a registered nurse (R.N.) or a licensed practical nurse (L.P.N.). Usually, physical therapy, respiratory therapy and other therapies also are considered to be skilled nursing care.

Intermediate Care

Intermediate care requires less than twenty-four hour nursing supervision. It is performed several times a week, or even on a daily basis, for stable conditions. This type of care must also be performed by, or under the supervision of, skilled medical personnel. Intermediate care refers to intermittent medical care, such as giving injections to the patient. The care is provided pursuant to a doctor's orders. Medicare may pay for care of this kind performed in your home.

Custodial Care

Custodial care is provided to help the patient function from day to day. Custodial care includes, but is not limited to, assistance with walking, bathing, dressing, feeding, and supervision over the administration of medicine. Essentially, custodial care is meant to assist the patient in meeting the *activities of daily living*, or ADLs (see also Chapter 6). The care might be provided in a nursing home, adult day care center, or at home.

Custodial care is provided to help the patient function from day to day. It does not involve daily continuous treatment of an illness, disease, bodily injury or condition. The person providing this care need not have medical skills or training. Custodial care is often referred to as *personal care*.

Long-term care policies frequently refer to these activities of daily living when determining eligibility for benefits. The policy stipulates that to receive benefits, one must be unable to perform a specified number of ADLs, such as bathing, dressing, moving from bed to chair, using the toilet, maintaining continence and feeding oneself.

SETTINGS FOR LONG-TERM CARE

In addition to these levels of care, it is helpful to look at settings of care. For the majority of people, the most desirable care setting is their own home. Staying at home allows them some independence and increases their quality of life. They maintain their autonomy to a certain extent and remain in control over their situation.

Home Health Care

Home health care is defined as medical and nonmedical services provided to ill, disabled or infirm persons in their residences. The home health care category covers skilled nursing care, as well as other services such as therapy or assistance with the activities of daily living. All of these levels of long-term care can be administered in the patient's home.

Medicare will only cover home health care that improves the patient's condition, rather than just maintaining it. As a general rule, it will not pay for nonmedical services. For example, Medicare's home health coverage will not pay for meals delivered to the home. The program also will not pay for homemaker services such as shopping, cleaning and laundry, nor will it pay for personal care such as bathing or helping the patient get dressed. These tasks are considered "custodial" in nature, meaning they can be provided by individuals who do not have medical training.

The only time Medicare will pay for home health care that is custodial is if it is directly related to treatment for an illness or injury. In these cases, Medicare will pay only if the custodial care is accompanied by skilled nursing care or therapy. Medicare will not pay for personal care provided by home health aides.

Coverage for home health care should be part of an individual's long-term care insurance policy. Sometimes it will be offered as a stand-alone policy. Although family members often provide nonmedical services for a loved one, some long-term care policies will not pay for services provided by family members.

Adult Day Care

As we all know, the home is not the only setting where long-term care occurs. Adult day care centers are another alternative. They provide activities and minimal health care during the day. The person in need of long-term care goes off in the morning and returns home at the end of the day.

But at some point, the individual who needs long-term care will not be coming home at the end of the day and will need to stay in a nursing home. A nursing home is the setting of care that many of us fear most.

Just Shoot Me: When a Nursing Home Is the Only Option Left

One woman sent the following letter to Ann Landers, the syndicated advice columnist: "My mother, a sweet little lady of 84, was in a nursing home after my father died unexpectedly. She needed round-the-clock care and supervision. Mom begged me daily to kill her. Once she tried to do it herself."

The letter went on to describe their last conversation. The mother continued begging for her daughter to kill her. The daughter pleaded that she could not, and that she would be put in jail if she did. The mother responded, "Then go to jail!"

Even though her mother died a short while later, the daughter felt tremendous guilt and sorrow that she did not fulfill her mother's last request.[2]

After visiting a relative in a nursing home, many of us have said half-seriously: "Just shoot me." We would rather die than find ourselves in that situation. Death seems less painful than confinement to a nursing home.

In a stand-up routine, a comedian pokes fun at the contemporary "hot" names for children, for instance Heather, Amber and Tiffany. "Someday," he says, "they'll be in a nursing home and you'll be hearing, 'Heather, Amber, Tiffany. Come take your medicine.'"

As the joke suggests, it seems incongruous to think of anyone named Heather, Amber or Tiffany in a nursing home. But in a few decades, we may see more residents of nursing homes with youthful-sounding names.

An article in *The Wall Street Journal* reported that the elderly are not afraid of aging. Rather, their biggest fear is being confined to a nursing home.[3]

In Florida, a glance through the newspapers could scare you even more. One lawyer advertises a seminar to discuss laws that protect nursing home residents. Here's a portion of the text from the ad:

"Everyday, residents of Nursing Homes suffer neglect and abuse at the hands of their caregivers. Often times, family members may live in another city or be able to visit only periodically. This puts family members at a huge disadvantage in questioning the quality of care their loved ones are receiving."

Another law firm ran an advertisement that is equally as frightening. It gives examples of problems that may occur in a nursing home that could give rise to a lawsuit. The examples cited included falls, infection, malnutrition, dehydration, bed sores, and inadequate care.

A different lawyer also hosts seminars on nursing home law. The attorney reports that he draws 80 to 100 people to his seminars. Ten years ago, the same seminar attracted only five or six participants.[4]

In Dallas, a jury awarded $10.7 million to the family of a woman who died after contracting gangrene in a nursing home. The jury found the nursing home to be grossly negligent in its care for the 80-year-old woman. The poor woman who died had suffered a stroke and could barely communicate. She was totally dependent upon the nursing home for all of her needs. The nursing home records showed that the woman had not been bathed for two days. As a result of the gangrene, the woman's foot was amputated and she died less than two weeks later.[5]

A few months later, a Florida jury awarded 6.3 million dollars in compensatory and punitive damages against a Boca Raton nursing home. The case arose after a retired high school principal suffering from dementia wandered out of a nursing home. The patient's body was found the following morning.[4]

Recently, the Arizona Supreme Court ruled that families of elderly persons who are abused by their caretakers may recover damages for the victims' pain and suffering. The ruling arose out of a lawsuit by the husband of a 74-year-old woman who suffered negligent and abusive treatment by nursing home employees. The suit alleged that the improper care caused dehydration, malnutrition and bed sores.[6]

On a regular basis, there are advertisements for lawyers who handle cases of abuse against the elderly in nursing homes. In some ways, these ads should be comforting, for they suggest that nursing home personnel will be fearful that an action may be brought against them if they are abusive. In other respects, the ads are disconcerting since they imply that many nursing home residents are victimized.

Sometimes, nursing home residents are victimized in other ways, besides neglect. Families of residents may discover that nursing home employees are stealing from the residents. A Memphis, Tennessee-based organization called Senior Crimestoppers has designed a program to prevent crimes in nursing homes. A national study conducted by the organization found that over 90 percent of residents and families have experienced theft in a nursing home.[7]

Sometimes, court-appointed guardians are the ones who victimize the elderly. A family member might even steal from an elderly relative. In one recent case, a woman's daughter was appointed guardian and was later accused of stealing hundreds of thousands of dollars from her own mother. The mother's attorney claimed the woman wanted an early inheritance and had figured out a way to do it.[8]

Usually, however, a child agonizes over how to care for an elderly parent. Children feel enormous guilt, because they are not taking a parent into their home. Although the fact may be that they do not have the time, skills or resources to care for a parent, that does not ease their guilt.

CHOOSING A NURSING HOME

No long-term care residence, whether it is a nursing home or an assisted living facility, is going to be right for some people. They have lived independently all of their lives and will never adjust to life in those circumstances. Still, when a long-term care residence becomes necessary for someone you love, you can at least make an informed, intelligent choice. Here are some items that you should consider:

- Licensed and/or certified
- Convenient location
- Special needs of patient
- Religious affiliation
- Availability
- Cost
- Staff and treatment of patients
- Environment; clean and safe
- Quality of food.

Ideally, the decision will be made for reasons other than money. One benefit of long-term care insurance is that it gives people the financial means to choose the best type of care, not the care that is the cheapest or that happens to be covered by some state program.

The goal in choosing the right nursing home is to provide the highest quality of life for the person in need of long-term care. You need to cut through the superficiality of the glossy brochures and the warm-and-fuzzy ads, and determine if residents are treated with dignity and respect. Ask friends, relatives and acquaintances if they are aware of a good nursing home in the area. Many times you will at least find out which ones to avoid.

First, "let your fingers do the walking." The official Medicare web site provides an excellent guide to choosing a nursing home (*http://www.medicare.gov/nursing.html*). Organizations in your state may provide guides that list all of the nursing facilities and personal care homes. The American Health Care Association in Washington, DC, can provide you with the affiliated state association that publishes this guide. Your state's Department of Aging, Health Department or Insurance Department might also have materials which list the residences in your area. Another option is to check the listings in the phone book for government offices in your county that deal with these issues. (See Appendices A and B.)

There may be legislation in your state which regulates nursing homes. These laws establish specific rights for nursing home residents. They also assure a higher quality of care and help enhance each resident's quality of life.

Pennsylvania's Department of Health maintains records on all nursing homes that are licensed in that state. These records are open to the public, and consumers can obtain annual inspection reports for the last five years, a licensure history dating back to when the nursing home opened, and reports based upon substantiated complaints filed within the past five years.

An agency in your state should be performing inspections of the facility. Ask to see those inspections, if they are not posted in a readily accessible place. Take note of what deficiencies are listed on the report. Also, check with state and local authorities to review any public records regarding complaints about the facility.

According to the Health Care Financing Administration (HCFA), the Federal agency that oversees Medicare and Medicaid, there are over 500 local ombudsman programs across the country. These ombudsman programs serve the aging and their families. Their goal is to assure the highest quality of care for the elderly. Although an ombudsperson is not permitted to recommend a particular nursing home, these men and women can provide the results of the latest survey, the number of outstanding complaints, the number and type of complaints filed in the past year, as well as the results and conclusions of recent complaint investigations. The ombudsperson can also provide general advice. You can find your ombudsperson by calling the National Association of State Units on Aging, at (202) 898-2578.

Many states have organizations that assist consumers in the choice of a nursing home. Usually, it's the state Department of Aging, the Health Department or a Long-Term Care Ombudsperson. They will offer booklets that can assist you in the choice of a nursing home. These publications will contain checklists for selecting a nursing home.

Some specific information to use to make the choice of a nursing home easier includes the patient-to-staff ratio, the number of registered nurses at the facility, special treatment available for Alzheimer's disease and other illnesses, as well as recreational opportunities for residents.

There are some basics in choosing a nursing home. The home should be conveniently located so that visiting will not be a nightmare. Adjusting to life in a nursing home will be a great deal easier if the resident is close to familiar surroundings and can visit family, friends, and doctors. If the person receiving long-term care cannot leave the facility, friends and relatives should try to visit frequently. At a nursing home in Pittsburgh, remodeling plans placed almost forty of the residents in jeopardy of being transferred to a facility across town. Needless to say, the relatives of the residents who chose that facility because of its location protested vigorously. Ultimately, the residents were not moved.

In making a search for the right residence, it is important to consider the special requirements of the person needing long-term care. Someone with Alzheimer's disease, for instance, may be best served by a nursing home that is equipped to deal with the special needs of a resident with that disorder. The area set aside for Alzheimer's patients should be secure, so residents don't wander off.

Some people want a residence that has a specific religious affiliation. These facilities are often run by a particular religious denomination. Normally, there is a place of worship within such facilities, and services are held on a regular basis.

Even if you do identify the perfect home, it may not be an option for you because it is filled. Some residences have a waiting list. If the projected wait is not too long and there is no immediate need, you can still keep that facility under consideration.

Unfortunately, you may need to rule out some nursing homes because of the cost. If the person in need of long-term care is relying on a government program to pay for care, the nursing home may not be willing to accept the individual. Find out what happens to residents if and when their money runs out.

You will need to make several visits to a facility to make an intelligent decision. When you visit, try to get a sense of the morale of the residents. That will not be hard if the residents look like zombies, staring at television sets for hours on end. Talk to relatives who are visiting and elicit their opinion of the facility. Ask hospital social workers, geriatric care counselors, and health care professionals about the nursing home's reputation as well.

While a tour of the residence with an administrator is a worthwhile and necessary endeavor, you need to conduct your own inspection of the facility. See for yourself if the residents are being treated properly. During your visits, listen to how the staff talks to residents —and not just when they know you are around. Visit at odd hours and on weekends to determine if the quality of care is consistent.

In addition to speaking with the administrator, talk to the director of nurses and other staff. Usually you can sense if they are caring individuals or if they hate working there. You will be able to judge whether staff members are patient, or if they are always frazzled. It will be a good sign if you find staff members who seem to enjoy caring for the elderly. A low turnover rate among employees is usually a good indication that the employees like their employer and their work.

Whenever you visit, the nursing home should be clean. There should be no obvious safety hazards. While you inspect the facility, it is not just what you see that should be of concern. If it smells bad, it is the wrong choice, too.

The food is another important part of the decision-making process. Ask the residents how they feel about the meals. While visitors can bring a salami sandwich that a relative craves, the food should not leave the resident saying, "Yo quiero Taco Bell," like the dog in the popular fast-food advertisement.

No matter what type of nursing facility it is, the thought of entering a nursing home is symbolic of losing our independence. Needing long-term care is much like becoming a child again. In my family, we joke about the prospect of needing long-term care, because it is too painful for us to think about directly. My wife jokes with my parents that when they can no longer cook for themselves, she will come over and do it for $500 per month. For $1000 per month, she will not subject them to her cooking.

Entering a nursing home, or placing a family member in one, is a gut-wrenching experience for everyone concerned. Nursing homes still have a stigma attached to them. Family members may feel extremely guilty and may fear that they will be perceived as selfishly putting their own needs ahead of the person being placed in the nursing home.

No matter how compelling the reasons are to put someone in a nursing home, the decision is one of the most difficult to make. When a nursing home is the only remaining option, most of us hope we will find the best care available for our loved one, no matter what it costs.

The Short Course on Long-Term Care Insurance

- *The "sandwich generation" has the responsibility of caring for aging parents while raising their own children.*

- *It is important to distinguish between levels of care and settings of care. The three levels of care are skilled nursing care, intermediate care, and custodial care. Custodial care is often referred to as personal care.*

- *All levels of care can be provided in the home. Medicare only provides limited coverage for home health care. It will only pay if the care is restorative in nature.*

- *Medicare rarely pays for custodial care. For Medicare to pay, the custodial care must be accompanied by skilled nursing care or therapy.*

- *Nursing homes are certified to provide different levels of care, from custodial to skilled nursing care.*

- *Your state may provide a wealth of information about nursing homes. The Department of Aging will have data available on nursing homes that will help you choose the right one for the person in need of long-term care. See Appendix B at the end of this book.*

Chapter 4

THE RISK OF NEEDING
LONG-TERM CARE

*I*n late February, 1998, a wire service story by Michelle Williams of the
Associated Press described the plight of Dr. Benjamin Spock, the author
of the famous books on how to raise children. Dr. Spock, who was 94 years
old at the time of the article, was unable to pay his medical bills. The article
was written after Dr. Spock's wife, Mary Morgan, sent out a letter to friends
and family, asking for help to offset his $10,000 per month in health care
expenses. Ms. Morgan told *The Boston Globe* that they were facing a severe
financial crisis because of the constant care he needed after his heart attack,
stroke and several bouts of pneumonia.[1]

Dr. Spock's wife indicated that insurance was covering only a fraction
of his medical bills. In a written statement, she estimated that Dr. Spock's
medical expenses would be $120,000 per year. She indicated that his home
care would include at least two full time helpers, special vegetarian foods,
equipment and yoga treatment. The woman pledged that she would never
send him away to be cared for and would always remain by his side.

Ironically, a literary agent estimated that Dr. Spock had earned an
inflation-adjusted $20 to $30 million in royalties from his writing. According to his wife, Dr. Spock's income in 1997 was $500,000. According to
her, much of it went to cover medical expenses, along with agents and
secretaries. The couple sold their home in Maine for $480,000 and moved
to LaJolla, California. In her statement, Dr. Spock's wife expressed hope
that others would learn from this example about how people should be cared
for at this stage of their life.

41

In response to Ms. Morgan's pleas that she could not afford to keep her husband at home, Dr. Spock's publisher promised to provide financial support. Sadly, however, Dr. Spock died soon after the report hit the newspapers.

Unfortunately, there are many people who want desperately to keep a loved one at home and who do not have the financial means of a Dr. Spock. They wish for a few dollars more in their paycheck to pay someone to help them care for their loved one while they go off to work.

It is not just 94-year-olds who need care. In South Florida, a 40-year-old man was in the final stages of melanoma. His wife had recently been laid off from work, and she had to find a new job to support her husband and their five-year-old son. Every time she went out for a job interview, the woman was forced to leave her husband writhing in pain on the couch. Even the strongest medication seemed to do little to ease his pain.

The woman was torn as she looked for work. Although they needed the money, she wanted to comfort her husband in the last months of his life. She wanted him to stay at home for as long as possible.

A recent study by the National Center for Health Statistics examining how Americans die revealed a great deal about the risk of needing long-term care. According to the study, one out of every ten people spends the last year of his or her life bedridden, due to illness. Half suffer mental or physical ills that restrict their ability to function. Fifty-six percent of people die in hospitals or other medical settings; 19 percent die in nursing homes.[2]

The study was conducted by examining more than 2.2 million death certificates. In addition, the researchers interviewed scores of survivors. The study, the first in more than a decade examining how Americans die, seems to show that the risk of needing long-term care is great.

Undoubtedly, long-term care insurance salespeople will offer the study as proof of the need for a policy. There is a saying in the insurance industry that policies are sold, not bought. And statistics like these will be used to market long-term care insurance.

To be fair, few people do understand the need for long-term care insurance. Whereas automobile insurance is required by law and homeowners insurance is required to obtain a mortgage, no one is forced to buy long-term care insurance. Nevertheless, the risk of needing long-term care is significant.

Consider these statistics: the risk of losing assets due to an auto accident is about 1 in 240. The risk of losing assets due to a fire in your home is about 1 in 1200. In comparison, however, three out of five people will need long-term care of some kind at age 75 or older. In fact, according to one national study, it is projected that 43 percent of adults who turned 65 years old in 1990 will be admitted for nursing home care at some point in their life.[3] One in three men who live to age 65 will spend three months or more in a nursing home. Fifty-two percent of women who are now 65 will spend their last days in a nursing home. Approximately one in four people will spend a year or longer in a nursing home. One in eleven will spend five years or more in a nursing home.

When long-term care is needed, a family's life savings can disappear in a hurry. The average cost of a year in a nursing home is $40,000. In more expensive areas that cost might double, depending upon the facility you choose.[4] Home health care can be every bit as expensive. Round-the-clock care of all kinds can run up an enormous tab.

Caring for someone who has been diagnosed with Alzheimer's disease will cost more than $213,000 over the individual's lifetime. This figure does not include all of the individual's medical expenses. Although Alzheimer's disease usually strikes the elderly, it can hit people when they are still in their early fifties.

Approximately half of all nursing facility residents pay the cost out of their personal resources.[5] Their care is financed out of income and savings, at least at the onset. A lifetime of savings may eventually be spent for long-term care.

The person in need of care will frequently become a burden, both financially and emotionally, upon family members or friends. Caregivers are faced with a great deal of responsibility as they support their children as well as their elderly parents. While coping with rising tuition bills, they are also dealing with escalating long-term care expenses. And, as the population ages, it will not be uncommon for senior citizens to be taking care of their elderly parents.

Bob Littell, an insurance broker in Atlanta, Georgia, believes his father's situation provides a good indication of the problem we may be facing. The senior Mr. Littell had his first heart attack in his fifties and another in his sixties. Later, he suffered from congestive heart failure, chronic obstructive pulmonary disease and several other medical problems. At age 85, he had triple bypass surgery.[6]

Littell's point is that in an earlier era, his father never would have survived long enough to need long-term care. As medical science advances, however, and more people are able to successfully undergo major heart surgery in their eighties, they will live much longer. The down side is that they will need long-term care.

The *New York Times* reported recently that living to age 100 is not so unusual anymore. According to demographers, there are 30,000 to 50,000 Americans over 100 years old, up from a 1980 estimate of 15,000. In fact, centenarians are the fastest-growing age group. By the middle of the next century, 800,000 Americans will live to be over 100.[7] Unfortunately, while Willard Scott's successor may be wishing you a happy 100th birthday on the *Today* show, someone else may be worrying about how to provide you with long-term care.

WHO PAYS FOR LONG-TERM CARE?

Many consumers are under the mistaken impression that Medicare pays for long-term care if it is needed. Yet Medicare only pays for about two to three percent of long-term care costs. Of all the nursing home care provided in the United States, only one-half of one percent is skilled care that is covered by Medicare. The care provided in most nursing homes is custodial care, which is not covered by Medicare.

Medicare will cover only skilled nursing care or skilled rehabilitation services in a Medicare-certified facility. Since most nursing homes in the United States are not Medicare-certified facilities, it logically follows that Medicare is not paying for this care. Medicare will not pay for custodial care, unless it is in conjunction with skilled nursing or skilled rehabilitation services.

Five conditions must be satisfied before Medicare will help pay for care in a Medicare-participating skilled nursing facility:

1. The individual needs daily skilled nursing or skilled rehabilitation services, such as cardiac rehabilitation;

2. The individual must have spent three days in a row in the hospital before being admitted to a participating skilled nursing facility;

3. The individual must be admitted to that facility within thirty days after leaving the hospital;

4. The individual must be receiving care in the skilled nursing facility for the same condition that he or she was treated for at the hospital; and

5. A medical professional must certify that skilled nursing or skilled rehabilitation services are needed on a daily basis.

Even if the patient meets all of those requirements, Medicare covers only the first twenty days in a skilled nursing facility. During the next eighty days, Medicare pays all but $96.00 per day. Most medigap plans (health insurance policies provided by private carriers that provide benefits not covered by Medicare) pay that co-insurance amount for days 21 through 100. Medigap plans usually pay the Medicare deductible as well.

As we have seen, there are significant holes in Medicare's coverage for home health care. As a general rule, Medicare will not pay for personal care and custodial services. Medicare will not cover homemaker services or housekeeping, it will not pay for meals, and it will not cover full time nursing care.

Policies which supplement Medicare only provide limited coverage for long-term care, although certain medigap plans do have at-home recovery benefits that pay a limited amount for at-home assistance with the activities of daily living for those who are recovering from an illness, injury or surgery.

MEDICAID

When all else fails, people who need long-term care can turn to Medicaid for coverage. Although Medicaid is a federal health program intended for the poor or medically indigent, it is managed by the states, and eligibility rules will differ from state-to-state. In your state, it may be called Public Assistance or Medical Assistance.

People applying for Medicaid to pay for long-term care are not likely to qualify until their savings are depleted and they have spent down their assets. Until they get to that point, they will be spending thousands of dollars each month for care. Nevertheless, there are "spousal impoverishment" provisions in the Medicaid law which offer limited protection for the spouse of someone who needs long-term. The spouse will be entitled to a monthly income or to a maximum stipulated by state law and is usually allowed to keep assets such as a burial plot, a car and their house.

Some individuals attempt to transfer their assets to a family member as a way to meet Medicaid's financial guidelines. The Omnibus Budget Reconciliation Act of 1993 (OBRA 1993) clamped down on such attempts. As a result of OBRA 1993, the "look-back" period on gifts and transfers was extended to thirty-six months. Consequently, gifts and transfers that were made within thirty-six months prior to entering a nursing home can jeopardize any entitlement under the Medicaid program. Under OBRA 1993, there is even a "look-back" period of sixty months on transfers to trusts established after August 10, 1993. Trusts are treated differently because they are much more complicated than an outright transfer and may be used to circumvent the Medicaid laws.

OBRA 1993 also requires states to attempt to recover payments made by Medicaid. In the past, these recovery decisions had been left up to each state to make. Although the spouse of a person who is in a nursing home usually will not lose his or her house, states must seek repayment of the amounts paid for long-term care by making a claim against the estate of the Medicaid recipient or of the Medicaid recipient's spouse.

Transferring assets to qualify for Medicaid creates an ethical problem for many people. In addition, many individuals feel there is a stigma attached to Medicaid. They view it as welfare and are reluctant to use the program.

The subject of Medicaid raises a host of issues that are beyond the scope of this book. A 1997 law was dubbed "Granny's Lawyer Goes to Jail." It imposes a prison term of up to one year for anyone who advises individuals to dispose of assets to become eligible for Medicaid. Many groups have criticized the law as a gag rule that criminalizes advice about asset transfers to qualify for Medicaid-financed nursing home care. A New York federal court has even refused to enforce the law.[8,9]

Despite the possibility of criminal penalties, there are attorneys who advertise they can help people qualify for Medicaid without losing all of their assets. They utilize Medicaid loopholes to transfer assets to relatives without violating the law. Many question the ethics of those maneuvers, saying that they are defrauding a program which was designed to help the poor. Some argue that Medicaid rewards people who could have bought long-term care insurance but did not.

Attorneys who specialize in Medicaid planning take a different position. They contend that long-term care insurance is a viable option only for healthy and wealthy seniors. Lower-middle class and middle class seniors cannot afford the premiums and should not be forced into poverty in order to qualify for Medicaid.

You should realize that transferring assets to qualify for Medicaid is dangerous for other reasons. By doing so, you may be cheating yourself out of receiving the best long-term care that is available. There is no guarantee that any money you turn over to your family members will be used to improve your quality of life. While the desire to not lose everything is understandable, it is your money, and you should be able to use it to make your final years as good as they can be.

Another very real problem is that many facilities do not even accept Medicaid patients or seek to get rid of the ones they have. On April 12, 1998, an ABC News report dealt with residents of a Vencor nursing home. Over two hundred residents who depended upon Medicaid for payment of their nursing home fees were kicked out, because the company claimed it was losing money on these patients. In response to the report, Vencor changed its policy and offered to readmit the former residents who receive Medicaid.

To prevent this problem from reoccurring, legislation was recently passed to bar nursing homes from evicting or transferring residents who rely on Medicaid for payment.[10] Homes that accept Medicaid reimbursement may not transfer or evict these residents to make room for individuals who pay out of their own pocket. Under the new law, nursing homes that convert to a private pay policy, which means they no longer accept people who rely on Medicaid for payment, must continue to house those who are already residents of the facility.

It is doubtful that Medicare or Medicaid benefits will be expanded in the near future. In fact, many legislators are advocating reductions in these benefits. As baby boomers age, there will be additional strain upon the system, making it unlikely that coverage for long-term care will broaden.

A positive development on the Medicaid front is the home and community-based services waiver program that is available in many areas. This is a waiver program that allows qualified individuals to receive care in their home, rather than in a nursing home. Some of the services provided include physical therapy, home health care, counseling, companion aid and personal care.

Generally, the person in need of care must be at least sixty years old and must choose to receive services in the home or other community setting. The services must not exceed eighty percent of the average Medicaid payment for a state nursing facility. The waiver program saves Medicaid funds and allows the individual to remain at home.

Another program to reduce Medicaid spending and to encourage the purchase of long-term care insurance is a partnership program. States establish partnerships with long-term care insurers. If an individual buys a partnership policy, he or she is allowed to shelter more assets if Medicaid is needed to pay for long-term care. Unfortunately, however, only four states (Connecticut, California, New York and Indiana) have established this program. The Connecticut Partnership for Long-Term Care only sold 7600 policies from April, 1992 through September, 1998.[11]

IGNORANCE IS NOT BLISS

Too many people think they have a safety net to fall back upon should the time come when long-term care is necessary. It is clear that the answer for most people is not Medicare, medigap policies or Medicaid. If you are reading this book, you probably are aware that one safety net that can help a lot of people is long-term care insurance.

A 1997 survey sponsored by UNUM Life Insurance Company of America and conducted by AgeWave, a business development company specializing in the needs of the aging population, revealed several disturbing findings. According to the survey, one in three people ages 40 to 70 believe they own long-term care insurance. In fact, less than one percent of the entire population, and less than six percent of the over 65 age group owns a long-term care policy.[12]

Worse yet, only 25 percent of those people surveyed recognized the product when it was described to them. Perhaps, before the next survey, you will have finished this book and will possess more than a minimal knowledge of long-term care insurance. Better yet, maybe you will have that knowledge before you or a loved one needs long-term care.

Key Points: The Short Course on Long-Term Care Insurance

- *One out of three people who live to age 65 will spend three months or longer in a nursing home. One out of four will spend a year or longer in a nursing home.*

- *Medicare has only limited coverage for long-term care. Medicare pays primarily for skilled nursing care, whereas most long-term care is custodial in nature, meaning the individual needs assistance with the activities of daily living. Medicare rarely covers custodial care.*

- *Medigap policies have extremely limited coverage for long-term care.*

- *Although Medicaid may eventually pay for long-term care, the individual has to spend down his or her assets to qualify. OBRA 1993 cracked down on individuals who transferred property and gifts in order to qualify for Medicaid. The "look-back" period is thirty-six months prior to entry into a nursing home. There are even criminal penalties that may be assessed against individuals who attempt to fraudulently transfer assets to qualify for Medicaid.*

- *Partnership policies, if available in your state, offer asset protection benefits if long-term care coverage runs out and the policyholder needs to apply for Medicaid.*

- *Although long-term care policies are relatively new, the market for them will continue to grow as aging baby boomers recognize the risk of needing long-term care.*

Chapter 5

IS LONG-TERM CARE INSURANCE RIGHT FOR ME?

The woman was already eighty years old before she started to worry about needing long-term care. She had no relatives in town and was afraid of spending all of her savings on long-term care. The woman quickly found, however, that peace of mind would not come cheap. A policy that would pay $80 per day for up to four years was priced at over $4000 annually. And there was a strong possibility that she would not qualify for the policy, even though her health was relatively good.

Unfortunately, buying a long-term care policy at age eighty is akin to purchasing homeowners insurance once your house is on fire. Although the premium is steep, you are still not a risk the insurance company is eager to cover. Seniors and their children should instead consider buying long-term care insurance at a much younger age. Although you may decide that a long-term care policy is unnecessary, every family should make an informed decision as to whether or not to buy the insurance.

According to a study conducted by the American Council of Life Insurance (ACLI), a person age 65 to 69 will pay an average of $2400 per year for an individual policy that pays for five years in a nursing home. Someone buying that same policy at age 75 will pay more than $5300 for the same coverage. The ACLI projects that a twelve-month stay in a nursing home will cost $190,000 in the year 2030.[1]

If you buy that same policy at age 35 to 39, the annual premium averages $507. The $507 per year is much less than what many people pay for auto insurance. Nevertheless, although a statistically high number of people are likely to need long-term care insurance at some point in life, the risk is remote at younger ages. Generally, younger people have more pressing matters to worry about —like raising children, paying tuition, making mortgage payments, and a dozen other expenditures that always seem to be arising.

Even when they are older, many people dismiss the possibility of needing long-term care. Looking younger is a more important priority. They do not give a thought to buying long-term care insurance.

HOW TO PAY FOR LONG-TERM CARE

If you are worried about having washboard abdominal muscles and looking ten years younger, nursing homes and long-term care seem an eternity away. It is hard for most people to plan for the day when they will be 85 years old and two years in a nursing home will cost almost $400,000. They are trying to make it to their next paycheck. Mind-boggling statistics about the cost of long-term care roll over their heads. It is much like someone saying that a loaf of bread will cost $10 someday. They will worry about that —someday.

But you are not the only one who needs to worry about needing long-term care someday. Maybe you are seeing your parents losing a step right now, and it is clear that they may need care in the near future. You may be the one who will be caring for them if they have not made provisions for the day when care becomes necessary.

Whether it is you or your parents who will need long-term care someday, it will not be cheap. And if the government is not going to pay for long-term care, how *do* you pay for it? If you have been putting money away toward this end, you may have a sizable amount to use to pay for care. If your assets generate a significant amount of income, you may be able to use the money to pay for long-term care.

Perhaps you are ready to liquidate assets to pay for care. If you are ready to sell your home, you might use the proceeds to buy into a continuing care or life care retirement community. As discussed in Chapter 2, they generally charge a one-time entrance fee as well as a monthly fee. The fees entitle you to an apartment, one or more meals per day, maid service, medical care, if necessary, and nursing home care, if required.

Maybe you will use your savings to pay to stay in an assisted living residence. Many are wonderful places to spend your final years and are a far cry from the facilities that gave rise to our negative perceptions of nursing homes.

If you are able to stay in your own home, another source of funding for long-term care is a reverse equity mortgage. Reverse mortgages permit you to draw cash from your house without making monthly payments. No repayment of the loan is required for as long as you live in the house. Under the most widely available reverse mortgage program, you must be age 62 or older to qualify. Unfortunately, with a reverse equity mortage, you will only receive a percentage of your home's market value. Normally this won't be enough to pay long-term care expenses. You are also using what may be your largest asset to pay for long-term care. The terms of these loans differ significantly from lender to lender.

The U.S. Department of Housing and Urban Development (HUD) can provide you with more information about reverse mortgages. They can be reached at: 451 7th Street S.W., Washington, DC 20410 (telephone (888) 466-3487) or through their internet site: *http://www.hud.gov.* Another excellent resource is the National Center for Home Equity Conversion, at 360 N. Robert, #403, Saint Paul, MN 55101 (telephone (651) 222-6775). They also provide information on reverse mortgates at the internet site: *http://www.reverse.org.*

WHY PURCHASE A LONG-TERM CARE POLICY?

One magazine article for insurance agents and brokers extolled the virtues of long-term care insurance. The authors offered several compelling reasons to buy long-term care insurance that might be used in a presentation to potential customers.[2] According to the article, these are the reasons why someone should buy a long-term care policy:

- To preserve financial independence;
- To avoid being dependent upon friends and relatives for care;
- To preserve freedom to make choices regarding care;
- To protect savings, assets and your standard of living;
- To conserve the estate and assure income for your spouse; and
- To avoid Medicaid.

A more objective source, the New York State Office for the Aging, advises that long-term care policies can help in the following ways:

- To protect your family from the catastrophic costs of long-term care;
- To remain in control of your own assets;
- To increase your chances of receiving your preferred choice of long-term care; and
- To maintain your own independence and dignity.

Between the two lists, there are a number of good reasons why a long-term care policy makes sense for many people.

WHO SHOULD PURCHASE A LONG-TERM CARE POLICY?

The fact is, more Americans are living longer. In the past fifty years, the odds of our living until age 85 have doubled, and our chances of living until age 85 will have tripled by the year 2000.

There is a down side to living longer. You are more likely to need long-term care. Increases in the average lifespan, however, have been followed by a worsening of morbidity statistics. It is estimated that conditions like senility, Alzheimer's disease and arthritis affect approximately twenty percent of the population over 65 and a sizable percentage of those who are over 85.

In another era, older individuals might have turned to family members for care in their sunset years. Today, however, the traditional family structure has changed. Family members may live across the country from one another. Two-parent households are becoming less common. Even in two-parent households, both parties often work outside the home and will be unavailable to provide care.

Traditional health insurance policies and Medicare offer little protection when the bill comes for long-term care. To fill that void, long-term care insurance has become more popular. Compared to other forms of insurance, long-term care policies are relative newcomers. In 1980, only a few long-term care products existed. Today, hundreds of individual contracts are offered and are being constantly revised. By 1986, only 200,000 had been purchased. By 1990, two million had been bought.

Unlike Medicare supplements (i.e., medigap policies), there are no standardized long-term care policies. Medicare supplements pick up some of the bills that Medicare will not pay. In all but a few states, there are ten standard policies, labeled A through J. A is a bare-bones policy, while J offers comprehensive coverage. However, not even Policy J is a substitute for long-term care insurance.

Although certain standard features are mandated by state and federal law, long-term care policies are frequently quite different from one another. When buying long-term care insurance, consumers must compare features between policies to see if they offer similar coverage. You cannot simply look for the policy with the cheapest price.

Buying long-term care insurance involves many trade-offs. For the policy to be affordable, buyers may need to decrease the daily benefit or the length of the benefit period. They might also need to extend the waiting period required before benefits begin.

In deciding whether to recommend long-term care insurance, some financial planners utilize a rule of thumb. If your assets amount to $250,000 or more, one planner recommends buying a long-term care policy. If you have less than $250,000 in assets, then you may be a candidate for Medicaid.

Other financial planners take a totally different approach. They advise that if you can afford to pay long-term care expenses on your own, you should not bother with long-term care insurance. These financial planners believe that if you invest what you would pay out in premiums, then you will be better off in the long run.

The United Seniors Health Cooperative, a nonprofit consumer organization, uses the following guidelines to determine if someone is a candidate to buy long-term care insurance:

- Each person in your household has more than $75,000 in assets;
- The annual income in your household is more than $30,000 per person;
- You can afford to pay the premiums without changing your lifestyle; and
- The premiums would still be affordable, even if they went up 20 to 30 percent.

Obviously, so-called "rules of thumb" are inadequate in many instances. Each individual's financial situation should be analyzed closely to determine if a long-term care policy is suitable. In fact, state insurance regulations sometimes require that the application for a long-term care policy address the issue of suitability.

The problem is that while "rules of thumb" work nicely in the abstract, they sometimes do not work when you apply them to the real world. The rule above will not pacify people who have worked all their life to accumulate assets and then lose everything to pay for long-term care. The assets they own are every bit as important to them as they are to people who have accumulated much more.

If someone hates the thought of going on Medicaid to pay for long-term care, the rules above are also meaningless. To many, accepting Medicaid is akin to going on welfare and it goes against their values. Furthermore, this rule is also meaningless if you do not believe that Medicaid will pay for the quality of care you would like to have if problems arise.

In contrast, some people might argue that it is more important for a person with less than $250,000 in assets to buy a policy than it is for the person who has more than that amount. In theory, someone with significant assets can afford to pay for long-term care without relying on a policy. The wealthier individual can put money aside in case the need for long-term care arises.

When you come down to it, a prescribed rule will not apply to many individual situations. There are people with less than $250,000 in assets and people with more than $250,000 in assets who would benefit from buying a policy. For either group, long-term care insurance might be advisable as a means to preserve their estate. In fact, some have referred to long-term care policies as inheritance insurance.

The prevailing opinion is that you should not buy a long-term care policy if it will cut into your current standard of living. Someone on a limited income should not buy a long-term care policy if it will adversely affect his or her lifestyle. One personal finance magazine suggests that a person should not spend more than five percent of his or her income on a long-term care policy.

As the United Seniors Health Cooperative makes clear, you cannot just look at the current premium and decide, "long-term care insurance is for me." Even if the policy is affordable now, the premiums may increase. The premiums for most long-term care policies are usually based upon the applicant's age when the policy is purchased, and younger applicants pay a lower premium. Nevertheless, it is possible that the premium may go up.

It might make sense for children to help pay for a parent's long-term care insurance. Otherwise, they might be compelled to provide long-term care for a parent, if it becomes necessary. Having long-term care insurance also helps to preserve the estate.

Aside from these financial considerations, family history is extremely important in determining who needs long-term care insurance. If there is a history of Alzheimer's or Parkinson's disease, then long-term care insurance might be in order, irrespective of the financial situation.

Lastly, assuming you can afford the premiums now and later, long-term care insurance should be purchased by someone who desires the peace of mind that a policy can bring.

WILL I BE ABLE TO BUY A LONG-TERM CARE POLICY?

Back in the eighties, when Gilda Radner was performing on "Saturday Night Live" and it was still a treat to watch this television show, her character called Emily Litella would rant and rave about assorted issues. With Jane Curtin sitting next to her at the news desk, Gilda would go on a tirade about "eagle rights" or some such topic. Finally, after letting her go on for a time, Jane Curtin would inform Gilda that it wasn't eagle rights, but *equal* rights. And Gilda would end with her famous, "Well, never mind."

Unfortunately, much of our discussion about long-term care insurance will be moot for some people. Even if you wish to buy a long-term care policy, you are not necessarily going to qualify. The 80-year-old woman mentioned at the beginning of the chapter was initially turned down by several companies, but not because of her age. She had a type of pernicious anemia that concerned the insurance companies, even though it did not cause her any problems.

According to research done for the Connecticut Partnership for Long-Term Care, over fifty percent of the people turned down for long-term care insurance eventually obtained coverage.[3] Some reapplied with additional information from their physician and were accepted. Others applied to a different long-term care insurer and were issued a policy. Each insurance company has its own underwriting standards, which leads to different decisions.

The *Women & Aging Letter*, a project of Brandeis University, suggests that if you are turned down, you should have the carrier send a copy of the medical reasons for denial to your doctor.[3] The physician may be able to correct any misunderstandings that may have led to the denial. Sometimes there may be incorrect information on file with the Medical Information Bureau (MIB), an organization that provides insurance companies with medical information about individuals.

One basis for denial that cannot be corrected is age. Usually, companies will not sell policies to individuals who are over a certain age. The *Life Association News'* 12th Annual Survey of Long-Term Care Insurance lists the age limit on purchasing policies. Commonly, the range is from age 18 years to age 84 or 85 years. Only a very few companies will sell you a policy up to age 99, while others stop selling policies to individuals who are over 75.[1]

You might even be too *young* to buy a long-term care policy. While some companies will sell a policy to an 18-year-old, others request that purchasers be at least age 45, age 50, or age 55. Most experts would agree that age 18 is way too young to worry about buying a long-term care insurance policy. On the other hand, you should consider making the purchase before age 55. That does not mean you need to decide to buy it, but you should give consideration to making the purchase.

No matter what age you are, you should not buy a long-term care policy without a full understanding of what coverage you are buying and whether it is necessary.

Key Points: The Short Course on Long-Term Care Insurance

- *There are no ironclad rules on who needs long-term care insurance. Generally speaking, individuals should not sacrifice their current standard of living to pay for a policy. Someone with very few assets really does not need a policy. Aside from the financial considerations, however, a policy would be advisable if there is a family medical history that puts them at greater risk of needing long-term care.*

- *Medigap policies are not a substitute for long-term care insurance.*

- *Even though certain features are mandated by state and federal law, long-term care policies differ from company to company. You must read the policy thoroughly to determine if you are getting the coverage you need.*

- *You may not qualify to buy a long-term care policy because of your age or a medical condition. Always find out the basis for the denial and follow up with the help of your doctor, if a mistake was made.*

Chapter 6

TRIGGERS AND TAXES

*I*f *you remember Trigger, Roy Rogers' horse, you are probably someone* who should consider buying a long-term care policy. Trigger and Roy are both gone, and none of us is getting any younger. As we age, the possibility of needing long-term care becomes less remote. Whether the policy is for you or for a loved one, it is imperative to gain an understanding of how one qualifies for benefits if care becomes necessary.

Before buying long-term care insurance of any kind, you must look at the policy triggers; that is, what conditions must be satisfied to receive benefits from your policy. Triggers in the long-term care policy govern whether someone is eligible for benefits.

Obviously, you would not want a policy that makes it extremely difficult to collect benefits. Usually, the lack of an ability to perform a specified number of the *activities of daily living* (ADLs) is the trigger which determines the benefits eligibility for a long-term care policy. If you can no longer perform the basic activities of living without assistance, you will qualify for benefits in most cases. Sickness is not a prerequisite, nor is a three-day prior admission to a hospital or acute care facility. The ADL standard recognizes that the need for long-term care often comes with age, not illness.

Usually, the state regulates insurance. In the case of long-term care insurance, however, Congress has stepped in with legislation. The Health Insurance Portability and Accountability Act of 1996 (HIPAA) created a tax break for purchasers of long-term care insurance and mandated that the benefits trigger in policies meet certain standards. HIPAA gave the same tax breaks to most policies purchased before January 1, 1997, even if their trigger did not meet the new standard. The Act also addressed other insurance issues, but they are beyond the scope of this book.

Under the Health Insurance Portability and Accountability Act of 1996, a long-term care policy must be "qualified" in order for the buyer to take a tax deduction; i.e., the policy must meet certain standards set forth in the Act for the policyholder to be able to deduct the premiums on their tax return. These standards were implemented to protect buyers of long-term care policies. Insurance regulators in your state may go even farther to protect consumers. Long-term care insurers usually offer contracts that are tax-qualified and contracts that are not.

Under HIPAA, to be tax-qualified a new policy must contain the following benefit eligibility standards. Long-term care services must be provided through a "plan of care" prescribed by a licensed health care practitioner. You must be diagnosed as "chronically ill." Triggers must be no more restrictive than the following:

- Due to disability or age, you are expected to be unable to do at least two of six activities of daily living without substantial help from another person for at least ninety days; or
- You need substantial supervision to protect your health and safety because you are cognitively impaired.

Under this law, the six relevant activities of daily living are considered to be:

- Eating
- Continence
- Bathing
- Toileting
- Dressing
- Transferring

Most of the ADLs are self-explanatory. Eating is the ability to feed oneself. Continence is the ability to control bowel and bladder function. Bathing is the ability to wash oneself. Toileting is the ability to use the bathroom and perform associated acts of personal hygiene. Dressing is the ability to put on and take off clothes, as well as any braces or artificial limbs. Transferring is the ability to get out of bed and into a chair or wheelchair and back.

The Health Insurance Portability and Accountability Act requires that a qualified policy have a trigger which utilizes these ADLs. To obtain benefits, the insured must meet the requirements stated above; that is, he or she must be unable to perform at least two out of six ADLs for at least ninety days due to a loss of functional capacity.

Under the Act, a qualified policy must have a second possible trigger that deals with needing substantial supervision to protect your health and safety, because you are *cognitively impaired*. Cognitive impairment means a deterioration in intellectual capacity characterized by a loss of memory, disorientation, and an impaired ability to reason. For example, an individual with Alzheimer's disease will qualify for benefits, even though he or she is able to perform all of the ADLs.

These triggers should stand alone. You are not required to satisfy both triggers in a qualified policy. If you have a cognitive impairment, the activities of daily living requirement is moot. Similarly, if you cannot perform two of six ADLs, there is no requirement of cognitive impairment. It is an "either-or" situation.

Although there is a federal standard for benefit triggers in a tax-qualified policy, a state may impose its own minimum standards on non tax-qualified plans. These may be the same or somewhat different. For example, the Wisconsin Insurance Commissioner's office allows non tax-qualified policies that pay benefits when a person cannot perform three or more ADLs. Therefore, if you live in Wisconsin, someone may be selling a non tax-qualified, long-term care policy with a trigger that makes it harder to collect. You would be much better off buying a policy which only requires you to be unable to perform two or more of the ADLs.

You can still find a less restrictive policy in Wisconsin, of course. Any policy in Wisconsin that is tax-qualified will have triggers which only require the inability to perform two or more of the ADLs. The point is that you should check carefully, or you may get stuck with a policy that requires inability to perform three or more of the ADLs to trigger coverage.

Some plans offer more favorable triggers to obtain benefits under a long-term care policy. A policy might only require that you be unable to perform one of the six ADLs, rather than two. Or, a trigger might be based upon a determination of "medical necessity," as certified by the policy-holder's physician. The medical necessity trigger is very subjective.

Some policies differentiate between ADLs and *instrumental ADLs*. Instrumental ADLs include cooking, grocery shopping, laundry, bill paying, taking medicine, telephoning and housekeeping. Some policies refer to instrumental ADLs in their trigger.

THE TAX RAMIFICATIONS

For many people, keeping their eyes open while they read about insurance is tough. When taxes are introduced into the conversation, they need to ask for a wake-up call from the front desk! Unfortunately, a discussion of the tax implications of buying a long-term care policy is unavoidable. The Health Insurance Portability and Accountability Act of 1996 offers a tax benefit to those who buy qualified long-term care policies. Making the premiums tax deductible induces people to buy long-term care policies. In theory, if more people buy a long-term care policy, there will be less of a strain on the Medicaid system. In this way, the law works to send a clear message that the government expects us to take greater responsibility for long-term care expenses.

Because of HIPAA, the premium you pay may be tax deductible. Beginning January 1, 1998, premiums paid for certain long-term care policies became deductible according to the following schedule:

Age 40 and younger	$ 210
Age 41 to 50	$ 380
Age 51 to 60	$ 770
Age 61 to 70	$2,050
Age 70 and older	$2,570

These figures represent the maximum amount you may deduct, even if your premium was much higher. This deduction will increase annually, based upon the medical care component in the Consumer Price Index.

At first glance, it does not seem that the government has given younger people much of a tax incentive to buy a long-term care policy. At the same time, younger purchasers of long-term care insurance pay a lot less for a policy. Consequently, there is justification for the differences in the limit on deducting premiums paid for a policy. Many long-term care insurers are lobbying for Congress to make premiums fully deductible.

However, just as you should not buy an investment simply because of its tax benefits, neither should you buy a long-term care policy only because it is a tax write-off. Furthermore, the deduction is not going to do many taxpayers much good. The premium you pay may not reduce your taxes by one cent.

First of all, buying a tax-qualified policy will not help taxpayers who take the standard deduction on their income tax return. If you do not itemize deductions, you will not be able to include premiums paid for a qualified long-term care insurance policy. Many buyers of long-term care policies no longer itemize deductions on their tax return. Their mortgages are paid off and they do not pay state and local taxes on wages. Often they take the standard deduction, so a tax write-off means nothing and it is not an incentive to buy a policy. In addition, anyone who does not have a mortgage or does not pay property taxes usually won't itemize deductions either.

Even if you do itemize, the deduction for medical and dental expenses is limited. You can only deduct the amount of your medical and dental expenses that is more than 7.5 percent of your adjusted gross income. Therefore, if your adjusted gross income is $50,000, your medical and dental expenses must be greater than $3750 before the premium for a long-term care policy begins to reduce your tax obligation.

Finally, as mentioned earlier, you are not able to include the full premium of a qualified long-term care policy in your medical and dental expenses. If you are 51 to 60, you can only include $770 in calculating your deduction. If you are 61 to 70, the limit on your deductible medical expense is $2,050. Again, you still have the 7.5 percent restriction.

To calculate your deduction, the IRS provides a medical and dental expense checklist in Publication 502. Long-term care expenses are considered to be medical expenses, as long as the provider is licensed. Therefore, you are not able to pay a friend or relative thousands of dollars for long-term care and include the payment as a medical expense.

If you have lots of medical expenses and exceed the 7.5 percent cap, the premium for a qualified long-term care policy will do you some good on April 15. In the context of long-term care, there are some other expenses to remember to write down. You can include the part of a life care fee paid to a retirement home that is designated for medical care. Therefore, if you are considering a life care community or a continuing care community such as those discussed in Chapter 2, some of those fees may be viewed as medical expenses. Nursing home expenses may also be included if the main reason for being in the nursing home is to obtain medical care. You can also include transportation for needed medical care. And, as stated above, you can include some of the premiums you paid for qualified long-term care contracts.

Even if the premium you pay for a qualified long-term care policy does not help your tax situation, the IRS still loves you. The bright side, if there is a bright side to collecting on any insurance policy, is that any benefits you collect are tax-free. Beginning in 1997, the IRS as a general rule has been treating qualified long-term care insurance policies as accident and health insurance contracts. Therefore, any money you receive from these qualified contracts, other than policyholder dividends or premiums, usually is not considered to be income and you owe no taxes on it. Check with an accountant if you run into this situation.

There are also tax advantages for employers who offer group long-term care insurance as an employee benefit. Long-term care insurance premiums paid on behalf of employees are deductible as a business expense, just as is the case for health insurance. Furthermore, if your employer pays all or part of the premium of a long-term care policy, it is not included in your income.

In some states there are additional tax incentives for employers and individuals relating to long-term care insurance. For example, Maryland grants a deduction against state income tax for employers providing long-term care insurance as part of the employee benefit package. Other states offer tax breaks in various forms to individuals who purchase long-term care insurance. The tax deduction is based upon the premium paid for long-term care insurance.

If you are the employee of a small business (50 or fewer employees) or if you are self-employed, ask your accountant about Medical Savings Accounts (MSA). There may be a way to pay long-term care insurance premiums out of your MSA and to reduce your tax burden at the same time. Your contributions to the MSA may be deductible. Much like an IRA, your contributions to the MSA may be invested and will grow in the account. No tax is due if withdrawals are made to pay for qualifying, out-of-pocket medical expenses, or for any reason after age 65.

COGNITIVE IMPAIRMENT AND ALZHEIMER'S DISEASE

During the presidential administration of Ronald Reagan, comedians made fun of his penchant for forgetting important events. Regardless of your opinion of the former president, it is sad to read that he has Alzheimer's disease. Newspaper accounts state that his wife, Nancy, is the only person he recognizes consistently. When Nancy is away, Reagan wanders through the house looking for her.

Closer to home, the mother of a good friend of ours suffered from Alzheimer's disease. For years, our friend's father attempted to care for her in the family home. The woman, an artist, began creating her paintings on the walls, instead of on canvas, and behaved bizarrely in other ways. Finally, our friend and his father brought her from Michigan to a facility on the outskirts of Pittsburgh. As far as we know, she is still being cared for in that facility, long after our friend has died of prostate cancer.

Alzheimer's disease is a progressive degenerative illness that affects the brain. The person's cognitive and functional abilities decline gradually over time. Some of the symptoms are memory loss, disorientation, impaired judgment, personality changes, mood swings and behavioral abnormalities. Alzheimer's disease affects ten percent of people who are age 65 and a much larger percentage of those who are 85 and older.

When people forget things, they joke about having Alzheimer's disease. In fact, Alzheimer's disease is nothing to joke about. Although the mind is gone, the body lives on. Even though their cognitive and functional abilities are deteriorating, their bodies may be strong and healthy. Sometimes the person stricken with Alzheimer's disease outlives all of the people who tried valiantly to provide care. According to one publication, the average length of stay in a nursing home for an Alzheimer's patient is 96 months (eight years). At a price of $40,000 per year, the care will cost $320,000.

A recent obituary summarized the accomplishments of a bright engineer with an impressive array of accomplishments. As an aside, the obituary mentioned that the engineer had fought a fifteen-year battle with Alzheimer's disease.

The family dealing with a relative with Alzheimer's disease faces enormous responsibilities. Each day, they must find the strength, time and financial resources to care for the individual. Caring for the person with Alzheimer's disease is a 24-hour-per-day job.

Fortunately, there are places to turn to for assistance. In most communities, there are support groups at churches, synagogues and public facilities. Adult day care and respite care can provide a well-deserved break if a family member is providing the care. Along with private facilities that provide adult day care and respite care, community-based organizations offer care on a daily basis.

One church provides care for $35 per day. A long-term care provider offers adult day care from 10:00 a.m. to 4:00 p.m. for $30 per day. Another organization offers adult day care for $35 and overnight respite care for $70. Usually, a hot meal and a snack are provided with the day care.

While these charges are quite reasonable, a typical family will be hard-pressed to pay these expenses for a long time. Assuming that adult day care will be utilized five days each week, and 52 weeks each year, the tab will be close to $10,000 every year. If the family requires respite care for weekends off or for a vacation, then the cost will be significantly more.

According to the California Registry's Online Senior Housing & Home Care Database, there are four types of facilities that can care for an Alzheimer's patient. These are:

- Retirement residences with assisted living programs;
- Small licensed residential care homes;

- Facilities that are dedicated to Alzheimer's care; and
- Nursing homes.

Nursing homes usually dedicate a particular area to Alzheimer's patients. Although they may do a good job of caring for patients, nursing homes are often chosen for financial reasons, not because of other preferences. Medicaid may be the only way to pay for the care, which leaves a nursing home as the only alternative.

Sometimes, nursing homes do not do such a good job of caring for Alzheimer's patients. In Lauderhill, Florida, an 86-year-old man was left outside the nursing home in brutally hot weather. His caregiver left him outside for at least two hours, clad in only his diaper. He died of heat stroke. Ideally, if long-term care becomes necessary for any of us, we will find a place where we are treated with dignity and respect.[1]

A long-term care policy is worthless if it does not cover Alzheimer's disease. You need a policy that covers cognitive impairment. You may be able to perform the ADLs, but must be reminded to do so. It is imperative that Alzheimer's disease be covered explicitly by the policy. Don't settle for the salesperson's assurance that Alzheimer's disease will be covered. See that it is specifically stated in the policy.

The time to consider buying a long-term care insurance plan is while you are still sharp. You will need all of your faculties to choose the best policy for the money. And, much like your tax return, if you cannot make sense of it, ask for help from professionals who deal with these issues and from people you trust.

Key Points: The Short Course on Long-Term Care Insurance

- *Buying a tax-qualified policy means that the benefit eligibility trigger will meet the federal standard. New long-term policies that are tax-qualified automatically contain features that protect the buyer. State-approved policies purchased prior to January 1, 1997 also provide the buyer with a tax break because of HIPAA.*

- *A tax-qualified policy will establish a trigger that is no more restrictive than the following:*

  - *Due to disability or age, you are unable to do at least two of six activities of daily living without substantial help from another person for at least ninety days; or*

  - You need substantial supervision to protect your health and safety because you are cognitively impaired.

- *Each trigger in a qualified long-term care policy stands alone. You only have to satisfy one, not both.*

- *With the trigger based upon cognitive impairment, it does not matter if someone can perform all of the ADLs. He or she can still collect benefits. This trigger protects Alzheimer's patients.*

- *Before buying any long-term care policy, go through the language dealing with benefit eligibility word by word. Make certain the agent explains it thoroughly and doesn't try to gloss over this issue.*

- *Although a policy is tax-qualified, it may not mean much when it is time to prepare your tax return. You can only deduct a portion of your long-term care policy premium. The premium you pay is subject to a cap that is based upon your age, and your deduction is limited to medical expenses that exceed 7.5 percent of your adjusted gross income. Usually, long-term care policies purchased prior to January 1, 1997 will also receive favorable tax treatment. If you bought a policy prior to that date, you may automatically be entitled to a tax break.*

Chapter 7

EVALUATING A POLICY

*B*uying *a tax-qualified long-term care policy is a way to ensure that the* benefits trigger and other features meet certain standards established by the government. However, this does not mean that all you need to do is choose *any* tax-qualified long-term care policy and you will be set. There are many other factors to consider before choosing a long-term care policy.

The process of buying a long-term care policy is not much different than the purchase of any product. Once you have decided you want to buy the product, you look for the features you want, the price, the company that makes it, and where to buy it.

Suppose you need a new television set. Initially, you would consider whether you ought to buy one with a 19-inch screen, a 25-inch screen, or a screen so big it engulfs your room. If you are a smart consumer, you investigate the companies that make the television. Perhaps you have had good luck with a particular brand, or you will research who makes the best sets by looking at *Consumer Reports*. Maybe you will buy it at a reputable store in your area where you have purchased television sets in the past, or maybe you will shop around. Another key factor in your purchase will be price.

Buying long-term care insurance is not too much different. You do not want just any policy, you want one that meets your needs. Just as with television sets, the company offering the policy is extremely important. In addition, you need to be able to trust the agent who is selling you the policy. You also want to be certain you are paying a fair price for the coverage.

This chapter discusses how to evaluate the policy you are buying and offers advice on getting the right policy for the right price. Chapter 8 describes some of the attractive add-ons which may be purchased as riders. Chapter 9 discusses how to make sure that the company selling it is reputable and dependable, and Chapter 10 provides some tips on finding an agent who will be able to help you find the right policy.

Generally speaking, buying insurance is not easy. Most people do not understand the terminology. Even when insurance companies attempt to make easy-reading policies, the language is still foreign to most people. The fact is, reading an insurance policy is not quite as exciting as reading a Tom Clancy novel. Clancy is a former insurance agent who switched careers after discovering that writing books was a little more fun than reading insurance policies for a living!

With other products, you know what features are important to you. With that television set, you know the size of the screen you want and you know that stereo sound is an important feature for your household. With long-term care insurance, you may have no idea what coverage is important.

TYPES OF LONG-TERM CARE POLICIES

Essentially, there are three types of insurance policies that pay expenses associated with long-term care. They are:

- Long-term care insurance policies;
- Nursing home insurance policies; and
- Home health care insurance policies.

Nevertheless, as we will discuss in Chapter 14, there are hybrid policies that also cover long-term care expenses.

Long-term care insurance policies cover institutional care, as well as care outside the nursing home such as home health care. Nursing home insurance policies only cover institutional care. Home health care policies normally cover care received in the community, such as home health care or other services like adult day care. Interestingly, in some states only policies that cover both institutional and community-based care may be advertised and sold as long-term care insurance policies.

One insurance company offers a policy that covers only care in a nursing home or in an assisted living facility, whether it is skilled, intermediate or custodial. The policy also offers coverage for care in a residential care facility, hospice facility as well as other settings. It also sells a home care only policy. Finally, it offers an integrated policy with full coverage.

The most comprehensive policy is usually the best choice. When purchasing coverage, your first choice should be to seek a true long-term care policy that covers care in an institution and in the community. Anything less than this in a long-term care policy narrows the protection you are buying, but a nursing home insurance policy is better than no coverage at all.

Unfortunately, although long-term care policies contain similar features, they are not standardized. A long-term care policy offered by one insurance company may be extremely different from another carrier's product.

MUST-HAVE FEATURES

According to Carol Einhorn, a long-term care insurance agent in Spring House, Pennsylvania, there are a number of "must-have" features to look for in a policy.[1] They are:

- No prior hospitalization required;
- Guaranteed renewability;
- Coverage for organic mental illnesses like Alzheimer's disease and senility;
- Waiver of premium under certain conditions;
- Waiting period of 100 days or less;
- Reasonable daily benefits;
- Adequate benefit period (three year average);
- Inflation protection; and
- Level premiums.

    Each of these features is discussed below.

Prior Hospitalization

At one time, you could not collect on a long-term care policy unless your nursing home admission was preceded by a hospital stay of three days or longer. The *prior hospitalization* requirement has been eliminated on newer policies. If you have an older policy, it is usually possible to eliminate this requirement by purchasing an endorsement to that effect.

If a policy were to require a prior hospitalization before benefits are paid, you could have a tough time collecting on it. For example, while someone suffering from Alzheimer's disease is likely to require long-term care at some point, it is doubtful that the person will need to be hospitalized prior to requiring care for Alzheimer's disease.

While I was working for the Pennsylvania Insurance Department, I saw a long-term care insurance policyholder miss out on receiving his benefits because of the three-day prior hospitalization requirement. The individual was in a hospital immediately prior to going to a nursing home, but not for three days. The long-term care insurer refused to pay even one dime under the policy.

Guaranteed Renewability

A long-term care policy would be worthless without a *guaranteed renewability* feature. Without it, an insurance company could cancel the policy if the insured became sick or is injured. These individuals would lose their coverage just when they need it most. When a long-term care policy is guaranteed renewable, it can only be canceled if you have exhausted the benefits or if the premium has not been paid. Furthermore, the company cannot raise the premium because your health has deteriorated.

A guaranteed renewable policy may be canceled only if all policies of that kind are canceled in the state. Usually, state insurance regulators must approve the cancellation. Guaranteed renewable does not mean that the premium will always remain the same, however. The premium can be increased as long as everyone in the state with that policy and in that rate classification receives a similar price hike. This rate hike must also be approved by insurance regulators.

A policy may be guaranteed renewable, but that will not help if the policyholder does not pay the premium. A *reinstatement provision* protects insureds who neglect to pay the premium. The insured, or someone acting on the insured's behalf, can seek reinstatement in certain situations that are stipulated by the policy.

Most states have regulatory safeguards in place to protect against an unintentional failure to pay the premium which is grounds for cancellation. Some policies include reinstatement provisions so that if an insured fails to pay the premium, the long-term care insurer must give notice to the insured and the insured's designee. Under the Health Insurance Portability and Accountability Act of 1996, you will get additional protection if you buy a tax-qualified policy. The policyholder may reinstate the policy for up to five months if the reason for nonpayment is cognitive impairment.

Some policies offer a *nonforfeiture benefit* as part of the package or for an additional fee. With a nonforfeiture benefit, policyholders continue to get coverage even if they stop paying premiums, similar to a paid-up policy. The policy will spell out the terms of the nonforfeiture benefit. It will probably require that the policy be in force for a specified length of time, and the benefits will be much less than they would have been if premiums had continued to be paid. Because you are not entitled to the full benefit, it is often referred to as a *reduced paid-up policy*.

Once again, your state insurance department will regulate the type of nonforfeiture benefit that is offered. For example, under Texas law, the insurance carrier must start providing nonforfeiture benefits no later than the end of the third policy year. Usually, the percentage of the benefit you will keep will escalate with each year that you pay the premiums on the policy. In Texas, you must reject the nonforfeiture benefit in writing, which is usually a sign that state regulators believe it is a feature that is worth serious consideration.

The *return of premium benefit* operates in a similar manner. Some or all of the premiums will be returned, if the policyholder drops the coverage after a number of years or dies. Companies normally charge a higher premium for this feature. Some experts argue that this allows people to hedge their bet and get back money if they decide this coverage is not necessary or that they cannot afford it. Others contend that you are paying more for the privilege of dropping the policy at a stage in life when there is a greater risk of needing long-term care.

With the return of premium feature, your beneficiary will be entitled to the refund if you die. Whether the premium is returned to you or a beneficiary, any claims paid under the policy will be deducted.

Coverage for Organic Mental Conditions

As was discussed, Alzheimer's disease is one of the most devastating illnesses that any of us may face. A policy would be worthless without coverage for organic mental conditions like Alzheimer's disease. Organic diseases are associated with an alteration in the structure of an organ, as opposed to a functional or psychosomatic disorder. Although Alzheimer's and Parkinson's diseases should be covered without restriction, there will be exclusions for other types of mental problems. The long-term care policy will not normally cover personality disorders or nervous conditions, for example. Diseases like Alzheimer's and Parkinson's are not limited to the elderly. Sadly, it was revealed recently that actor Michael J. Fox is undergoing treatment for Parkinson's disease.

Waiver of Premium

Many policies offer a *waiver of premium* feature as part of the policy or as an option. This feature permits you to stop paying premiums once the insurance company has begun paying benefits. There may be limitations on this provision; for instance, it may not apply if you are receiving home health care. If you are at the point where you qualify for benefits under a long-term care policy, then paying long-term care insurance premiums is a burden you do not need.

Waiting Period of 100 Days or Less

The elimination period is the waiting period before benefits begin. It is much like a deductible on an auto insurance policy or the waiting period for benefits to begin on a disability insurance policy. The elimination period has a significant impact on the premium. Extending the waiting period for benefits to begin will decrease the price of the long-term care policy.

It is important to consider how long you can afford to wait for your benefits to begin. Since the cost of long-term care may be thousands of dollars per month, an individual can run up a high tab in a short time. Selecting the right elimination period is a balancing test. If you take more risk on your own shoulders by extending the waiting period, you will pay less premium. Similarly, if you accept an elimination period of 90 days or longer, you will pay less premium for a long-term care policy. If the care costs $36,000 per year —or $3,000 per month— you might be on the hook for $9,000 or more. Nevertheless, if you do not buy a long-term care policy because it is too expensive, you will lose a lot more than $9,000 if you need care at some point.

While having a short waiting period means little out-of-pocket expense if long-term care is needed, it can also cause the premium to skyrocket. In order to cut costs, the buyer might select a lower daily benefit or a shorter benefit period.

Many financial experts view long-term care insurance as protection against catastrophic losses. They believe it pays to take a longer elimination period to extend the duration of the benefits.

Insurers offer many different elimination periods, from zero days to a hundred or more. Twenty, thirty, sixty, ninety, or 100 days are a few of the more common options. If you have a plan with a twenty day elimination period, the company will begin paying benefits on the 21st day. Depending upon the age of the applicant for long-term care insurance, certain elimination periods will not be available.

One approach to selecting the right elimination period is to look at what Medicare covers. Medicare covers the first twenty days in a skilled nursing facility. During the next eighty days, Medicare pays all but $96 per day.

The problem with this approach, however, is that long-term care is not necessarily preceded by a hospital admission or care in a skilled nursing facility. There is no guarantee that Medicare or that a medigap policy will cover any of the elimination period. Remember again that Medicare and medigap policies rarely pay for long-term care expenses. The buyer of long-term care insurance should be prepared to pay the bill for the entire elimination period.

Although it is unusual for someone to go in and out of a nursing home, it is still important to look at how the policy treats subsequent admissions to a nursing home. Some insurers require a second elimination period, even if you are readmitted within a short amount of time. Many companies, however, will view the second stay as part of the first one if you are readmitted within a specified amount of time, such as thirty days. Some policies only require that the elimination period be satisfied once in the insured's lifetime. You should be able to purchase a policy with a once-in-a-lifetime elimination period as a standard feature.

Reasonable Daily Benefit

Choosing the right benefit is a very difficult task. The daily benefit must be compared to the cost of long-term care that may become necessary. Long-term care policies pay a daily rate of anywhere from $50 to $500 per day. The *Life Association News*' 12th Annual Long-Term Care Insurance Survey found that maximum daily benefit provisions have risen, mainly due to inflation.[2] More companies are now offering $250 to $300 maximum daily benefits.

A policy with a benefit of $100 per day pays roughly $36,500 per year toward long-term care expenses. An $80 per day benefit will pay approximately $29,000 per year. While that benefit may be adequate now, it might be insufficient in subsequent years when long-term care costs escalate.

Insurers require minimum daily benefits or minimum amounts of coverage that must be purchased. A company might require that the home health care benefit be a specified percentage of the nursing home coverage. Normally, it is fifty percent of the nursing home benefit. Therefore, the policy that pays $100 per day would usually contain a $50 per day benefit for home health care.

Typically, policies pay benefits based upon either actual expenses incurred or on an indemnity basis. The actual expense policy pays the actual charge for eligible services. Even if your daily benefit is higher than the actual charge, the policy only pays the actual bill. An indemnity policy pays the selected daily benefit, even if the actual charge is less. With both policies, the benefit is paid directly to the insured, unless it is assigned to the provider of long-term care.

With "integrated" or "pooled" benefits, payment is not allocated to one particular level of care. You have the option of using the benefit for any type of care that is needed. With some long-term care policies, benefit dollars are pooled together to form a benefit account. When you need care, the cost is deducted from your total benefit. This type of policy lets you use care that costs less than the maximum daily amount and to conserve coverage. Benefits are available until every dollar in the account is used. Even with the pooled benefit, however, the company will usually not pay above the maximum daily amount. Nevertheless, some policies permit the person in need of care to draw from the policy's pool of money to pay expenses without a daily benefit maximum.

A good way to choose the benefit level you need is to look at nursing facilities in your area and find out the cost. Check out the cost of adult day care and of home health care. You will at least have a rough idea whether the benefits you are buying are adequate for right now. Later in this chapter we will look at inflation protection to ensure that the coverage will be adequate down the road.

You can get by with a lower daily benefit if your other income, such as a pension, will pick up a portion of the long-term care expenses. Let's say you purchase a $100 per day daily benefit. Over a typical thirty day month, it will provide $3,000 to cover long-term care. You can use your other income to pay for long-term care expenses in excess of that amount.

What Levels of Care are Covered?

When you are selecting a daily benefit, make certain it applies to all levels of care. The long-term care policy should offer coverage for skilled nursing care, intermediate care, custodial care, adult day care, and home health care. Some insurance companies offer stand-alone home health care policies. Chapter 13 addresses home health care policies specifically.

Many policies do not distinguish between levels of care. The policy pays a daily benefit for any long-term care that is needed, as long as the eligibility requirements are met.

It is not enough to know what levels of care are covered. The policy may limit the types of facilities where the services are performed. Some policies will not pay for custodial care in a particular type of facility, even if it is licensed by the state to provide that kind of care.

The better policies do not restrict care to a nursing home. They allow for community-based care like adult day care or care in an assisted living facility.

One major long-term care policy offers coverage for care in a variety of settings. The policy covers:

- Nursing and therapy in the home;
- Care or assistance with daily activities in the home;
- Homemaker or companion services;
- Personal care attendant or chore services;
- Care or assistance received in a community-based setting;
- Adult day care;
- Assisted living facility care;
- Adult congregate living facility care;
- Alternative care facility care;
- Hospice care; and
- Nursing home care.

This particular policy offers a different approach to coverage for long-term care. It combines the preferred provider concept with a long-term care policy. Although policyholders still can choose who will provide long-term care, the company offers a provider network. If you use a provider from the network, you will receive a preferred rate for care and service. The provider, which claims to have a continuum of long-term care facilities, guarantees access to care.

Adequate Benefit Period

When buying a long-term care policy, a benefit period must be selected. The benefit period dictates how long benefits will be paid. A benefit period can last anywhere from one year to the lifetime of the insured. In an ideal world, people could afford to buy a policy that will pay benefits for life. In the real world, however, the cost of that policy would be prohibitive for many people. Trade-offs must be made to avoid paying a premium that is beyond their means.

In Texas, the minimum benefit period you can buy is one year. Benefit periods are usually one, two, three, or five years, or for the lifetime of the insured. Some long-term care insurers provide a maximum benefit, rather than a benefit period. If you purchase a lifetime benefit of $100,000, the long-term care policy would pay until the maximum benefit has been exhausted.

In deciding what benefit period to purchase, there are many factors to consider. Statistically, the average length of stay in a nursing home is 2.5 years. Nevertheless, do not forget some of the frightening statistics mentioned earlier dealing with the duration of care for Alzheimer's patients.

The age of the insured is also an important factor. At certain ages, the insured is more likely to die than to need long-term care for too long.

Another consideration is how long it will be until Medicaid picks up the cost of long-term care. Some financial planners suggest a benefit period of thirty-six months, which is the usual "look-back" period for Medicaid. The individual can transfer assets to a family member and can utilize the long-term care insurance for three years until he or she qualifies for Medicaid. Once again, if the thought of using Medicaid is unpalatable, you do not need to take this issue into consideration.

As a general rule, the benefit period for home health care coverage is shorter than for other levels of care. The policy may have separate limits such as five years for a nursing home and two years for home health care. In addition, home health care coverage will have additional limitations. It may only cover payments to certain providers such as nurses, therapists or licensed health aides. Chapter 13 addresses home health care in greater detail.

Inflation Protection

Alan Greenspan, the Chairman of the Federal Reserve Board, is not the only one who needs to worry about inflation. A long-term care policy is not going to do you much good twenty years from now if your benefit is the same as it is today. More than likely, without protection against inflation, the policy is likely to be completely inadequate.

Inflation riders add significantly to the cost of long-term care insurance, but they help the policy keep pace with the escalation of nursing home and other costs. With an inflation rider, the daily benefit increases by a fixed percentage each year for a specified period. The lifetime maximum increases proportionately as well.

The compounded inflation rider increases coverage more rapidly than does the simple inflation rider. With the compounded inflation rider, the daily benefit increase grows larger each year.

The adjustment with a simple inflation rider is a fixed percentage of the original daily benefit. When the adjustment is compounded, the daily benefit grows each year and the increase is based on the higher amount. The concept is similar to compound versus simple interest in a bank account.

Typically, an inflation rider on a long-term care policy will increase the amount of coverage by five percent each year. A $100 per day daily benefit will become $105 at the policy's anniversary date. With a simple inflation rider, the daily benefit will increase by $5 each year. With a compounded inflation rider, you will get more coverage each year. Instead of the five percent being based upon the original daily benefit of $100, it will be based upon the higher amount of coverage at each anniversary date of the policy. Your increase in coverage will be five percent of the increasingly higher amount. After the benefit is increased to $105, the next increase will be five percent of $105 (to $110.25), and so forth.

Buying inflation coverage is extremely important, especially if you are relatively young and may not be using the policy for a long time. A nursing home that is $100 per day now may cost three times that much in ten or twenty years. One expert believes that refusing inflation protection only makes sense if you are over age 75.

Adding inflation coverage to your policy is not cheap. Essentially, you are buying additional coverage each year. The cost of inflation protection is dependent upon your age at the time the policy is purchased. According to the Health Insurance Association of America, inflation riders can add 30 to 90 percent to your premium.

A special report on long-term care insurance published in *Consumer Reports* suggests that agents are reluctant to sell inflation coverage.[3] Agents are afraid that the additional premium will scare off potential buyers of long-term care insurance. Jesse Slome, editor of *Long-Term Care Insurance Sales Strategies*, has found that only one-third of long-term care policies includes inflation protection.[2]

Nonetheless, state regulators consider inflation coverage to be extremely important. In many states long-term care companies are required to offer inflation coverage. Furthermore, if you decide not to buy it, your rejection must be in writing. This is one way for regulators to ensure that you were offered this protection but turned it down.

Frankly, you are better off buying a policy that has inflation protection, rather than one that simply lets you buy more coverage in the future. The option to buy more coverage winds up being more expensive. Instead of the premium being dependent upon your age at the time you bought the policy, you will pay for coverage at the rates in effect at the time you increase the benefit. No proof of insurability is required. In contrast, with an inflation rider, the premium is based upon your age at the time you buy the policy.

Level Term

With most long-term care policies, the premium is based upon your age at the time of purchase. In contrast, with an attained-age policy, the premium goes up as you grow older. You are far better off with a policy where the premium you pay is based upon your age at the time the policy is purchased. Younger people pay less for the policy. Older people pay more. Studies show that it pays to buy the policy at a younger age. You will have the coverage for a longer time, yet pay less in premiums over your lifetime. There is also the risk that if you wait too long to buy long-term care insurance, you may not be healthy enough to be eligible for coverage.

Even though a policy is guaranteed renewable, the cost will not always remain the same. Therefore, the premium is not level in the traditional sense. For that reason, the National Association of Insurance Commissioners has objected to the use of the word "level" in conjunction with the sale of a guaranteed-renewable policy.

Assuming you do not have an attained-age policy, once your premium is determined, it can only be increased if a rate hike for everyone in your rate class is approved. Your rate class stays the same, even if your health deteriorates over the years. Your premium will not change unless state regulators approve a rate hike for everyone who was in your rate class at the time you purchased the policy.

RATE INCREASES

The peace of mind you get from having a long-term care policy does not always give you comparable peace of mind with regard to the price you have to pay. Consider the following scenario: one Friday evening, you come home to a letter from your insurance company, saying that the price of your policy is going up. For someone who is on a fixed income, this is always bad news. Worse yet, your agent is gone for the weekend and the insurance company is also closed.

It would be bad enough if the price went up five or ten percent, but the letter states that the premium is going up 25 percent. The long-term care insurer expresses its regret, but it is not sorry enough to cancel the rate increase. The letter assures customers that it worked diligently to avoid a much larger increase. Each page of it is filled with facts and figures on why the increase was necessary. The letter explains that the state insurance regulators approved the increase.

This story has already happened to many long-term care policyholders. And the rate increase might be more than 25 percent. Even if the policy premium is based upon your age at the time of purchase, someday you may get a rate increase.

As a rule, insurance regulators hate to approve rate increases. It means angry calls and nasty letters from consumers. The consumers also call their state representatives who apply pressure on the regulators. Rate increases mean a lot of flack for the state employees who oversee the sale of insurance in your state.

However, the people who regulate insurance fear that if they do not grant a rate increase, the long-term care insurer will run into financial problems. If an insurance company goes belly-up, it causes problems for everyone. While there may be a guaranty fund in your state that protects you if an insurance company becomes insolvent, guaranty funds do not provide all-encompassing protection. Furthermore, insolvencies undermine the stability of the guaranty fund.

With most long-term care policies, the price you pay is based upon your age when you buy the policy. It is one of the selling points used by the agent. "Buy it now," the agent will say, "And you will lock in the price forever." The agent will not draw attention to the fact that the policy may go up if a rate increase is approved for everyone who shares your classification. Therefore, the premium is not level in the classic sense.

Because long-term care insurance is a relatively new product, insurers do not have sufficient underwriting data to predict the number of claims that may come at a later date. Long-term care policies have what is known as a "long tail," which means the claims will not come in for many years. Indeed, the person buying the policy may not file a claim until decades later.

In a popular insurance magazine, an insurance expert posed a rather frightening scenario. He wondered what would happen if virtually all long-term care policies turn out to be drastically underpriced once the aging population begins using them. This dangerous situation is a possibility because we are living longer. Instead of dying, more people are likely to live, but may need long-term care.[4]

The author of the article suggested that many carriers have stayed out of the long-term care insurance business, because they fear the unpredictable potential exposure. As medical science finds ways for us to live longer, the risk of needing long-term care becomes greater. Therefore, the period for which long-term care is needed might double or triple over the next ten to fifteen years.

Bob Littell, the Atlanta insurance broker who wrote the article, fears that prices may double or triple in the future —and that is in addition to cost-of-living adjustments. He notes that some state insurance regulators have already begun placing caps on allowable premium increases. His concern is that this will force rates upward on new business and might lead to more claims being denied by the long-term care insurer.

One solution, the author suggests, is to convince 45- to 60-year-olds to buy long-term care policies. Another is to develop long-term care products that offer asset accumulation, much like the cash value in a whole life policy. Younger adults would be more likely to purchase them if the policy offered cash value and protection.

When rates go up significantly, long-term care policyholders are left in a difficult position. They may just be reaching the point when needing long-term care is likely. Furthermore, since the premium is based upon age at the time of purchase, the customer cannot simply switch companies, for the premium at the new company is likely to be even higher than the amount charged by the insurance company that has just increased its rate. In addition, the customer might not be healthy enough to qualify for a policy at a different company.

Thomas Foley, the Life and Health Actuary for the North Dakota Insurance Department, feels strongly that rate stabilization should be the number one goal during the design, pricing and sale of long-term care policies.[5] Foley believes that peace of mind is the reason people buy insurance. If long-term care policy premiums are not stable, peace of mind is eroded. In addition, since seniors are usually on a fixed income, they often cannot afford rate increases.

Some states have laws and regulation which ensure rate stabilization. In Wisconsin, the premium cannot be increased during the first three years of the policy. After the initial three years, any rate increase is guaranteed for at least two years after it becomes effective. For insureds who are 75 or older and for whom the coverage has been in effect for at least ten years, then the rate cannot be raised by more than ten percent.

DETERMINATION OF THE POLICY PREMIUM

The premium for a long-term care policy will be based upon either issue age or attained age. Premiums based upon attained age increase automatically as you age. Most often, however, the premium is based upon your issue age. With this type of premium calculation, the amount you pay is based upon your age at the time the policy is purchased. Younger people pay less for the policy. Older people pay more.

The premium for most long-term care policies will be based upon your rate class at the time of purchase and, in theory, the premium won't go up. The rate class you are in is dependent not only upon your age, but also where you live and your health at the time the policy is purchased. You will also pay less if you are a nonsmoker. Once your rate class is set, it will not change, even if your health deteriorates.

Studies show that it pays to buy the policy at a younger age. You will have the coverage for a longer time, yet pay less in premiums over a lifetime. There is also the risk that if you wait too long to buy long-term care insurance, you may not be healthy enough to be eligible for coverage. According to the United Seniors Health Cooperative, a nonprofit consumer organization, you will pay three or four times as much for the same policy if you buy it at age 75 as opposed to age 55.

The latest Health Insurance Association of America (HIAA) Survey[6] compared annual premiums for individual policies with a $100 per day nursing home benefit and a $50 per day home health care benefit. The policies compared provided four years of coverage and a twenty day elimination period. The average annual premium was as follows:

$ 247	Age 40
$ 364	Age 50
$ 980	Age 65
$3,907	Age 79

According to the HIAA Survey, the average annual premium for the same policy with a 5 percent compounded inflation feature was as follows:

$ 589	Age 40
$ 802	Age 50
$1,829	Age 65
$5,592	Age 79

SHOP AROUND

As with any policy, prices for similar coverage differ from company to company. Each company uses its own underwriting system to determine the premium and there is a wide disparity in pricing. Therefore, it pays to shop around for the best price among reputable and financially-stable companies. Nevertheless, some experts recommend avoiding a policy that is drastically cheaper than all of the others with similar features. If a policy is too cheap, it may be a tip-off that the coverage is not what it appears to be or that the insurer does not have an accurate idea on what to charge. It might even mean that the insurance company is more likely to resist legitimate claims. Either case might cause problems down the road.

Key Points: The Short Course on Long-Term Care Insurance

- *The long-term care policy should specifically cover Alzheimer's disease. Personality disorders, nervous conditions and other mental problems may be excluded.*

- *Long-term care is not necessarily preceded by a hospital stay. Therefore, the policy should not require a prior hospitalization to be eligible for benefits. Very few policies written today require a prior hospitalization to be eligible for benefits.*

- *A guaranteed-renewable policy is one that cannot be canceled, unless you stop paying the premiums or exhaust your benefits.*

- *The premium for a guaranteed-renewable policy can be increased, but only if everyone in that rate class gets hit with the same increase. State insurance regulators usually must approve the rate increase.*

- *Inflation riders are extremely important, especially if you are relatively young and long-term care costs continue to escalate. Nevertheless, inflation protection is quite expensive. Instead of an inflation rider, a less desirable alternative is an option to buy more coverage on a guaranteed-issue basis at the market rate.*

- *You can reduce the price of your long-term care policy by lengthening the elimination period, which is the time you must wait for benefits to begin. Even though it may be costly to suffer through this waiting period, a longer elimination period makes the policy more affordable. Extending the elimination period is much like raising the deductible on your car insurance. You agree to take responsibility for some of the risk.*

- *Although the premium of a long-term care policy is based upon your age at the time of purchase, it can still be raised. Rate increases require the approval of insurance regulators in your state. The rate may only be increased if everyone in your risk classification receives a rate hike as well.*

- *If you can barely afford long-term care insurance now and your income will remain relatively constant, you risk having to drop the coverage if there is a rate increase at some point. You should not purchase long-term care insurance believing that the premium will never go up.*

- *When comparing prices, always compare the exact same coverage from company to company. In your comparison, make certain you are using the exact same elimination period, daily benefit, and benefit duration. Like other forms of insurance, it pays to shop around for the best price.*

Chapter 8

BELLS AND WHISTLES

*A*bout fifteen years ago, my wife and I were shopping for a new car. Neither of us is interested in automobiles and shopping for them is an activity we both dread. When it comes to cars, my wife cares about the color, and I'm concerned with price. After we finally chose a car, people at work quizzed me about the size of the engine and asked a lot of other questions. Other than the price of the car, I really didn't know much about it. When my friends asked why we chose that particular car, I answered that it had several convenient coffee cup holders.

As it turned out, we really enjoyed owning that car. Nevertheless, even though it turned out to be a good car, buying an automobile because of the beverage holders is not too smart. Similarly, there are numerous "bells and whistles" that may attract you to a long-term care policy, but which should not be the basis for your decision to buy it.

Chapter 7 discussed how the price of a long-term care policy is determined. Comparing the cost of the same coverage from policy to policy is the best way to shop for the best price. Unfortunately, that is not always easy, because policies are not standardized.

Long-term care insurance is not as clear-cut as medigap coverage, for instance, which has ten standard coverage programs. No two long-term care policies are exactly alike. You can buy the same benefit period, the same elimination period and still have different policies. Also, unless you buy a tax-qualified policy, even policy triggers may differ. The home health care coverage may vary from policy to policy. Some companies offer benefits for different settings of care, such as assisted living, respite care and adult day care.

To further complicate matters, some companies include certain coverage as part of the basic policy, while others add the same coverage through riders. While sometimes a rider or endorsement can add valuable coverage, other times it can limit the coverage that is available. It is risky to assume that a rider is just a nonessential extra that really adds nothing of value to the policy. The key is choosing between meaningful coverage and the extras that really add no value to the policy.

As we saw before, inflation riders are extremely important as a way for the policy to keep pace with escalating long-term care costs. In fact they are considered so important that some states require the purchaser of long-term care insurance to specifically reject the inflation rider. The inflation rider will, however, also add significantly to the price of a policy.

For another example, sometimes you will need a rider to add home health care coverage. As discussed, home health care coverage is an extremely important benefit, especially if you hope to remain in your home for as long as possible. Even when home health care benefits are provided only through a rider, it is extremely important to purchase this coverage.

With so many long-term care products to choose from, insurance companies attempt to distinguish themselves and their products from one another. As companies develop new products, they will also add all types of "bells and whistles" to entice you to buy them.

Yet, try not to be distracted by these attractive add-ons. First it is most important for you to establish the basic coverage you need and to price the same coverage from a number of companies. Then you should consider those extras that are important to you.

WHAT ADDITIONAL FEATURES ARE WORTH BUYING?

LAN's 12th Annual Survey of Long-Term Care Insurance Policies asked companies about the additional benefits they offer in conjunction with long-term care policies. Some of the additional benefits listed in the various policies are:

- Adult day care
- Alternate plan of care
- Respite care
- Ambulance
- Bed reservation
- Restoration of benefits
- Nonforfeiture
- Caregiver training
- Care coordination
- Care advisory service
- Equipment purchase/rental
- Nonprofessional/family care
- Emergency alert system
- Prescription drugs
- 10-year paid-up option
- Guaranteed purchase
- Single premium paid up option
- Shared benefits for spouse
- Spousal discount.

Depending upon the company offering the policy, these additional benefits will be called by different names. Often they will be included as part of the basic policy. In some instances, you will need to pay extra to obtain this coverage. Another confusing factor is that certain benefits are spelled out specifically, while others may be covered under a broader category such as "alternate plan of care."

In some policies, coverage for an alternate plan of care refers to assisted living, adult day care and/or respite care. It might cover a type of living arrangement that does not even exist today. As part of the alternate plan of care benefit in some policies, the insured has access to a health care professional who will develop a plan to care for the individual.

The alternate plan of care might include modifying the person's house so that the individual can remain at home. The amount paid to the contractor for remodeling the dwelling is then deducted from the lifetime benefit. Benefits paid in this way might be limited to a percentage of the lifetime benefit, such as 60 percent.

Generally, this alternate plan of care benefit includes non-conventional care and services that may not be covered specifically by the policy. Martin Weiss, chairman of Weiss Ratings, Inc., warns that insurance agents may overstate the value of alternate care plans.[1] According to Weiss, this benefit is only as good as the insurer's willingness to use it. If the language is vague, the insurance company may interpret the benefit in a way that limits its value.

You might compare the situation to managed care. Ideally, the primary care physician will select the best treatment for the patient without consideration of the cost. However, as we all know, the expense of the treatment is often a very important factor in the doctor's decision.

Read the alternate plan of care language carefully. Do not assume that it is a catchall for all the benefits that the policy is missing. The key is to look at the outline of coverage, rather than relying on the salesperson's assurance that a particular type of care will be covered.

Many of the add-ons pointed to by the salesperson are extremely worthwhile, but they should not be the basis of your decision to buy a particular policy. For example, a long-term care insurer will sometimes offer a ten percent discount on both policies, if both you and your spouse apply for coverage and are accepted. Obviously, if you are not married, the salesperson is not going to make a big deal out of this perk.

Yet, even if you are married, that does not necessarily mean that both you and your spouse need a long-term care policy. Only one spouse may have a particularly bad medical history that warrants the purchase of a policy. If there is no need for both of you to have a policy, then do not let the agent use this feature to sell you an unnecessary policy. In addition, Weiss warns that most companies only offer the discount if you and your spouse purchase identical policies. But a husband and wife may not need identical coverage.

A husband and wife might be interested in the *shared benefit* option offered by some long-term care insurers. With this option, there is a single benefit account, but it can be accessed by both spouses. Unfortunately, this option will not let you buy two policies for the price of one. The policy has a total benefit that applies to all insureds under the policy. If one insured collects benefits, the amount paid is subtracted from the total policy benefit, usually on a first come, first served basis.

The *bed reservation benefit* option holds the insured's nursing home bed, if he or she must be moved temporarily to a hospital. Usually, the benefit pays up to thirty days per year. Otherwise, the insured might not have a room to come back to after a temporary hospital stay. Remember that the nursing home may still charge, even if the resident is in the hospital.

The *restoration of benefits* option lets you dip into your long-term care policy more than once. If you use the long-term care benefits for less than the original contract and go for a specified amount of time without using additional services, your policy will be restored to its original form. This feature will not help many people, since it is unlikely they will be going in and out of a nursing home.

A policy should offer other benefits like *respite care*, which assists the primary caregiver. This benefit allows the primary caregiver to take a well-deserved break from tending to the patient. The policy pays up to the maximum daily benefit for alternative care during the primary caregiver's absence. Frequently, the cap is 21 days of respite care. One policy even pays $500 toward training the caregiver.

Some insurers offer an *informal caregiver benefit* option. They will pay homemaker/companion benefits to family members who provide these services to insureds. Many long-term care insurers resist offering this type of benefit. They fear the benefit will be abused and they will be billed for services that were never rendered. These insurance companies believe this situation is ripe for fraud and will not reimburse a relative who is providing long-term care to the insured.

Some insurance companies offer *free care management* to purchasers of certain plans. The advice is provided so policyholders can maximize the benefits for a longer period of time. In contrast, other companies will deduct care management services from your benefit account.

One insurance company announced in a trade magazine that policyholders in Arizona and North Carolina may be able to participate in its "Productive Aging" program. After buying a policy, you have access to qualified advisers who can offer advice, information and referrals. These advisers help the family make decisions about long-term care.

Buyers of another company's long-term care policies are entitled to use what it calls its "LTC Connect" service, which offers discounts on prescriptions, vision care and hearing-related expenses through participating providers. The discounts range between 20 and 50 percent. The service is available to group and individual long-term care policyholders at no extra charge.

Some long-term care policies offer a *nonforfeiture benefit* as an extra. This benefit can take many different forms. When you purchase this option, you or your estate will be entitled to a return of premium if the policy is not utilized during your lifetime. Another form of nonforfeiture benefit permits policyholders to continue to get coverage, even if they stop paying premiums. It is similar to a *paid-up* policy. Many companies offer a ten-year paid-up option. Chapter 7 discussed nonforfeiture benefits.

Each specific policy will outline the details of the nonforfeiture benefit. It will probably require that the policy be in force for a specified length of time and the benefit will be much less than it would if you continued paying the premium.

One company's nonforfeiture benefit option works in the following manner. If you cancel coverage or stop paying premiums after the policy has been effect for at least three years, the policy will continue with a benefit account equal to all the premiums you have paid or 30 times your daily nursing home benefit, whichever is larger. If your daily benefit is $100 per day, the amount not forfeited would be $3,000 or the total amount of the premiums already paid. The company makes money by investing the premiums. It may be years until it pays out the $3,000. You are also paying extra for this option.

Some nonforfeiture benefits provide for a premium refund upon death. The policyholder's estate is entitled to any premiums paid, less any benefits that were used during the insured's lifetime. Obviously, the insurance company has no intention of returning the money it made by investing those premiums over the years.

No matter what type of nonforfeiture benefit it is, the company will usually charge a higher premium for this feature. According to the National Association of Insurance Commissioners, nonforfeiture benefits can add 10 to 100 percent to your premium.

While some of these extras may be useful to you someday, they should not be the reason you decide upon a particular policy. Bells and whistles should only be considered if you are having difficulty choosing from between two or more equally-good policies that cost a similar amount.

Key Points: The Short Course on Long-Term Care Insurance

- *Determine the essential coverage you need and price that same coverage from a number of companies.*

- *Do not let the salesperson use "bells and whistles" to distract you from the main substance of the policy. While there are many features that could be useful additions to a policy, they should not be the basis for your decision to buy a certain policy.*

- *Riders are not just a way for the insurance company to jack up the price of a policy. Riders and endorsements help you tailor the policy to your specific needs. Frequently, important coverage is added to the policy with riders, such as inflation protection.*

- *Long-term care insurers may give with one hand and take with the other. The policy may boast that long-term care is monitored by a care coordinator; i.e., a medical professional who supervises the insured's care. However, some carriers charge for this service and deduct it from the policy benefit.*

Chapter 9

EVALUATING AN
INSURANCE COMPANY

*T*he plot of John Grisham's novel, The Rainmaker, *revolves around a* lawyer fighting an evil insurance company that routinely denied legitimate claims. While Grisham's novel is fiction, many people actually believe that this is the way insurance companies operate. In reality, insurance products are tightly regulated by the states and it is doubtful that insurers could get away with the unscrupulous behavior described in the book. In addition, the unethical insurance company would be besieged by lawyers who do not have Grisham's talent for writing best-selling books.

Nevertheless, bad insurance companies do exist. Some insurance companies do look for ways to deny claims. They will seize upon any language in the policy to deny a claim. They rarely give customers the benefit of the doubt.

At some companies, the culture emphasizes selling at any cost. There is enormous pressure on salespeople to sell a policy, even if the customer does not need it. The emphasis is on sales, rather than on service.

On the other hand, there are many fine insurance companies that do not exploit customers. They offer valuable products at a fair price. These insurers are in business for the long-term and their reputation is important to them. When it is time for a customer to file a claim, they are waiting to help and will respond quickly. Their decisions are fair and reasonable. The trick is identifying which companies these are.

Normally, you might ask friends, relatives, or business associates about their insurance company. Unfortunately, these individuals are unlikely to have a long-term care insurance policy, and probably will not be able to give their thoughts on a particular company. You will not be able to find as many people who have bought long-term care insurance as you would with auto, homeowners or health insurance, and it will be tough to get a first-hand recommendation.

FINDING A COMPANY YOU TRUST

If you are shopping for a long-term care policy, it is important to find a company you trust. Perhaps you are very satisfied with the insurance company you are with now. You might want to see if it offers long-term care insurance. Unfortunately, it is quite possible that the carrier does not sell long-term care insurance, since it is a relatively new product.

According to *LAN*'s survey, 46 different companies offer 101 group and individual long-term care policies. Although there are a lot more choices for traditional types of insurance, there are still enough companies in the marketplace that sell long-term care insurance so that making a decision is difficult.

Many cities have groups whose purpose is to counsel older citizens about issues related to long-term care. Such a group may be affiliated with your state's health department or the department of aging, and may be found by contacting that agency (see Appendix B). In addition, every state has an insurance department or some agency that deals with insurance-related problems (see Appendix A). If you call your state's department of insurance, you may be able to get valuable information on long-term care insurers. The department of insurance may have a list of companies offering policies in the state or may be able to send you guides dealing with the purchase of long-term care insurance. Your state's insurance department may even have a Web site that is filled with valuable information on this topic.

Some state insurance departments may not be able to reveal specific information about a particular insurer. For example, insurance department employees are sometimes prohibited from revealing whether a particular company has generated complaints. Nevertheless, the insurance departments of other states are able to provide this kind if data. The Texas

Department of Insurance will provide a written company profile which shows the insurer's history, complaint record and financial rating. The Department's Internet Complaints Information System is also a valuable resource (*http://www.tdi.state.tx.us/consumer/icis/icis1.html*).

The Pennsylvania Insurance Department offers consumers a report that provides detailed information about companies doing business in that state. The report includes customer service contacts, Web sites, ratings, financial history and a three-year complaint history for insurers doing business in Pennsylvania. The report also provides a complaint index that lets consumers compare companies.

Other states publish a complaint ratio for companies doing business in that state. The ratio compares the number of complaints filed with the number of policies written in the state. Unfortunately, the complaint ratio is usually based upon auto and homeowners insurance. It is not likely to tell you much about companies who sell long-term care insurance. Even if statistics on long-term care insurers are kept in your state, they are likely to be of minimal value, since claims will not show up for a number of years.

The mere fact that a company is licensed by the state insurance department is not a guarantee that you are dealing with a reputable company. The list of long-term care insurers provided by the Department of Insurance in Arizona, for example, includes a disclaimer. It states that the list is not all-inclusive and does not represent an endorsement by the Arizona Department of Insurance.

INSURANCE COMPANY RATING SERVICES

With long-term care insurance in particular, the financial rating of the company is of the utmost importance. You should choose a financially stable company that will be in existence when it is finally time to file your claim.

Although complaint records are not normally available, your state's insurance department may be able to supply the financial rating of the insurer you are considering. Nevertheless, the state insurance department does not analyze the financial strength of the insurance company itself. There are a number of independent services that do such ratings.

Rating Service	Phone Number and Website	Rating System (Best to Worst)
A. M. Best	(800) 424-BEST (800) 420-0400 *http://www.ambest.com*	**Letter grade:** *Secure:* A++ Superior A+ Superior A Excellent A- Excellent B++ Very good B+ Very good *Vulnerable:* grades below B+ to F (in Liquidation) **Financial Performance Rating (FPR):** *Secure:* 9 Very Strong 8, 7 Strong 6, 5 Good ***Vulnerable:*** 4 Fair 3 Marginal 2 Work 1 Poor
Standard & Poor	(212) 208-1527 *http://www.ratings.standardpo or.com*	**Financial Strength Ratings** AAA Extremely Strong AA Very Strong A Strong BBB Good Vulnerable: BB to CC
Duff & Phelps Credit Rating Company	(312) 368-3157 *http://www.dcrco.com*	**Claims Paying Ability:** AAA AA+ AA AA- A+ A A- BBB BB+ BB etc.

Rating Service	Phone Number and Website	Rating System (Best to Worst)
Moody's Investor Service, Inc.	(212) 553-0377 *http://www.moodys.com*	**Financial Strength** Aaa Exceptional Aa Excellent A Good Baa Adequate Ba Questionable B Poor Caa Very poor Ca Extremely poor C Lowest
Weiss Ratings, Inc.	(800) 289-9222 *http://www.weissratings.com*	**Financial Health** A Excellent F Failed

One of the most prominent independent rating organizations is A. M. Best, although there are several other companies that provide an independent opinion of an insurance company's ability to meet its obligation to policyholders (see Table). Although a few highly-rated companies have run into financial problems, the rating systems can be extremely helpful in evaluating the financial strength of an insurance company.

A. M. Best assigns two types of rating opinions, a letter grade ranging from A++ to F or a Financial Performance Rating (FPR) ranging from a high of 9 to a low of 1. The letter grade represents an opinion which is based upon a comprehensive quantitative and qualitative evaluation of an insurance company's financial strength, operating performance and market profile. The FPR is A. M. Best's opinion, based upon a quantitative evaluation of a company's financial strength and operating performance. As a general rule, FPR ratings are assigned to small or new companies.

Under the A. M. Best rating system, A++ is the top grade. It means the carrier has a superior rating. A+ is also a superior rating. A and A- are considered to be excellent ratings. B++ and B+ are very good ratings. A++ through B+ are viewed as Secure Best's Ratings. Grades below B+ are classified as Vulnerable Best's Ratings.

In lieu of the letter grade rating, a company will receive an FPR rating. An FPR 9 rating is the highest and is indicative of a very strong company.

FPR 8 and FPR 7 are strong; and FPR 6 and FPR 5 are rated good. A. M. Best classifies these FPR 9 through FPR 5 Ratings as secure. However, ratings below 5 are considered vulnerable. FPR 4 is viewed as fair, FPR 3 is marginal, FPR 2 is weak and FPR 1 is considered poor.

When you are shopping for a long-term care policy, insist on a company with a secure rating from A. M. Best. The higher the rating, the better off you are. If I were buying the policy, I would select a company with a letter grade of A+ or better.

When you buy a long-term care policy, you are looking at receiving benefits decades from now. Perhaps you are in your fifties and will not need the policy until you are an octogenarian. It is in your best interest to buy a policy from a company that has been in business for a lengthy period of time. If a company is too new or too small to have a rating from A. M. Best, it is a much riskier bet for the purchaser of long-term care insurance.

To find a company's rating, you can visit the A. M. Best web site at *http://www.ambest.com*. The rating can be sent to you by fax or e-mail. There will be a minimal charge for each Best's Rating. You can also contact A. M. Best at (800) 424-BEST to obtain ratings for a fee. Before paying for this service, however, check with your local library to see if the ratings are available without having to purchase them. A good business library will have the latest book with A. M. Best ratings.

There are several other companies that rate the financial stability of insurance carriers. Standard & Poor's Insurance Rating Services' grades range from AAA to CC. As of May 11, 1998, Standard & Poor's changed the method by which it rates insurance company. The "claims-paying ability" was replaced with "financial strength" ratings. Standard & Poor's top rating is AAA, which means the company is extremely strong. AA means the insurance company is very strong and the A mark reflects that the carrier is strong. Companies with a BBB rating are considered to be in good financial shape. However, ratings from Standard & Poor that fall below BBB mean that the company is considered vulnerable.

Standard & Poor's ratings are available at website *http://www.ratings.standardpoor.com*, and phone (212) 208-1527. You can also find them in your local library.

Duff & Phelps Credit Rating Company in Chicago offers reports on insurance companies, too. Although it still utilizes a Claims Paying Ability, the rating is a good indicator of an insurer's financial strength. The rating you should look for is AA or better. Insure.com (formerly the Insurance News Network) also provides the Duff & Phelps rating for many major companies. The phone number for Duff & Phelps is (312) 368-3157. The internet address is *http://www.dcrco.com.*

Another place to look is Moody's Investor Service, Inc. When looking at the Moody's rating, you should expect to see an Aa or better rating. The number for Moody's is (212) 553-0377, and the internet address is *http://www.moodys.com.*

Weiss Ratings, Inc. can also be used to research the financial health of the insurer. Weiss Ratings, as a general rule, provides the most skeptical report on the insurance company's financial well-being. The rating service can be reached at (800) 289-9222 or on the internet at *http://www.weissratings.com.*

States usually have a guaranty fund that will make good on the policies of licensed insurance companies that have become insolvent. Nevertheless, these guaranty funds do not offer the same protection as you get through the Federal Deposit Insurance Corporation (F.D.I.C.) and the Federal Savings and Loan Insurance Corporation (F.S.L.I.C.) These organizations protect you if your bank or savings and loan goes under. Coverage through a guaranty fund is not as good. If your long-term care insurer goes under, the guaranty fund will not necessarily put you back in the same position that you were prior to the insolvency.

Be wary of an agent who explains away the financial rating of the company backing the long-term care policy by saying that you are protected by the state guaranty fund. Do not ask for problems from the get-go. No one should do business with a company that is experiencing financial problems, even if that is the only coverage available.

Also, do not rely upon the salesperson to tell you the ratings of the companies from which you are buying a policy. Often, your state's insurance department can provide the financial ratings of long-term care insurers. Due to limited resources, however, that department may not have the latest ratings or might not be able to supply them at all. As mentioned above, a good business library will have the A. M. Best and other ratings for most insurance companies.

You want to be certain that an insurance company is committed to selling long-term care insurance. It is conceivable that once the aging population begins utilizing long-term care insurance, some companies will begin losing money and will get out of the business. Look for a company that has been selling long-term care insurance for a number of years and has hundreds of millions of dollars in policies. Make sure they are selling products across the country and not just in a particular area.

The financial rating of a company is important for another reason. A long-term care insurer that is struggling financially may be more inclined to turn down legitimate claims. For the financially-troubled insurance company, claims drain more cash than it can afford to lose.

Key Points: The Short Course on Long-Term Care Insurance

- *Always contact your state's insurance department to determine what information is available on long-term care insurers. The insurance department can usually provide a list of the companies who sell policies, as well as the financial rating of the company. Only deal with licensed companies who have been in business for a significant length of time.*

- *When buying a long-term care policy, your first choice should be a company with an A+ or better rating from A. M. Best. Even if there is a guaranty fund in your state, the independent rating of the company is extremely important. Also, always check with at least one other rating service besides A. M. Best (see Table).*

- *Contact the long-term care ombudsperson in your state or an Area Agency on Aging. Aside from the insurance department, there are state agencies that deal with issues of the elderly that may offer advice on which insurers offer the best policies.*

Chapter 10

HOW TO FIND A
RELIABLE AGENT

When I worked in consumer services for the Pennsylvania Insurance Department, a woman called with a complaint about an insurance salesman trying to bully her into buying a long-term care policy. The agent was pushy and would not stop calling her. When I asked her to file a formal complaint, the woman was reluctant to do so. I could not understand why until the woman mentioned one detail she had previously neglected to tell me: the agent was her son-in-law. She did not know how to refuse to buy a policy without causing a rift in the family.

One would think that having an insurance agent in the family is an ideal situation. You have someone you trust who knows about insurance. It would seem that a family member would never sell a relative anything less than the best policy. But that is not the way it works in real life.

Sometimes, greed is thicker than both water *and* blood. Many insurance companies teach agents how to "prospect" for clients. Agents are taught to make lists of everyone they know, including relatives. Their first days are spent calling people on that list, attempting to sell them policies. After honing their skills on friends and relatives, they graduate to making "cold calls," which means telephoning people they do not know at all.

While still with the Pennsylvania Insurance Department, I received a call during lunch hour from an agent who sold long-term care policies. The agent called to ask the financial rating of long-term care insurers, so he could use them in a presentation to clients. Although an agent should have access to these ratings through other means, I looked them up for him, even though I was the only one available to answer phones at lunchtime.

After finding out the ratings of five companies and giving them to the agent, he asked for more information. The list of five companies soon became ten. The other telephone lines started ringing, and I asked if I could call him back with the additional ratings. However, the agent would not hear of it.

I put the other calls on hold, while attempting to fulfill the agent's request. After providing a few more ratings, I asked again if I might call him back after answering the questions on the other lines. The agent became more insistent. His tone was belligerent.

Finally, I decided enough was enough. I asked his name and phone number. Although the agent provided his name, he brusquely told me not to bother calling him back and hung up without a "thank-you."

I marked down the agent's name and put it in my desk. It did not stay there long. The next day, I got a call from an elderly woman who was in tears. She claimed that an insurance agent had badgered her into buying a long-term care policy. The woman stated that he was rude and told her he would not leave until she bought the policy. The woman swore he pressured her into buying the insurance.

Surprisingly, or perhaps not, the agent she complained about was the rude and aggressive agent who had called our office for financial ratings. Further investigation showed there were other complaints against him.

Every state has an agency that investigates complaints against insurance companies and insurance agents. Usually, it is called the insurance department and it is run by the insurance commissioner for the state (see Appendix A). The job of each state's insurance department is to enforce the insurance laws that are on the books.

Insurance regulators look for patterns of complaints against agents and insurance companies. Often, the same names keep showing up on their desks. Most insurance department employees are genuinely interested in helping consumers and in controlling bad agents and companies. Even though the results may not be to a consumer's liking, it is always important to file a complaint if you believe you were victimized. If complaints are not filed, the insurance department will not be able to establish a pattern of deceit or misconduct.

Unfortunately, state insurance departments are often underfunded and lack the resources to police all of the unethical insurance activity in their state. Whereas this particular long-term care salesperson quickly became known as someone who intimidated customers, many unethical salespeople get away with these improper sales tactics for years.

State insurance regulators have a great deal to say about what policies are offered in the commonwealth. Regulations pertaining to the sale of long-term care policies will usually be very strict, since most buyers are older and potentially more vulnerable to unethical agents and insurers. Nonetheless, the fact that a policy is approved by the regulators in your state is no guarantee that the policy is a good one. The policy may meet only the minimum standards required by insurance laws and regulations.

For example, regulators may require a minimum loss ratio on policies sold in the state. The loss ratio is the amount paid out in claims compared to the premiums charged. In many states, long-term care policies must have a loss ratio of at least sixty percent. At least sixty cents out of every dollar collected in premiums must be paid out in claims. The purpose of minimum loss ratio regulations is to protect consumers from companies that pay out very little in relation to the premium they charge.

A state will also require certain forms to be completed by the customer and the agent when a policy is sold. Specific questions must be asked to protect consumers against unscrupulous agents and insurers. For example, the application for long-term care insurance will question whether the coverage is appropriate for this individual. In addition, state insurance regulators may require a compounded inflation rejection notice which the insured must sign if he or she wishes to reject the rider. The inflation rider was discussed in earlier chapters.

State regulators will usually impose a *policy delivery receipt requirement*. The purchaser of the policy signs a form documenting that the policy was received. If you do not receive your policy within 45 days, contact the company. Always pay for your policy by check or money order and not with cash. Make the check payable to the insurance company.

Your state's insurance department might also require that a form be filled out if the new policy is purchased as a replacement for another one. In general, regulators believe that replacement is always good for the agent but is not necessarily good for the person buying the policy. Agents like selling new policies, even though a person's old policy is adequate. With a new sale, the agent gets a sizable commission and potential bonuses from the company writing the policy.

State regulators may also control the commissions and compensation paid to agents. In some states, the agent's compensation on the sale of long-term care policies is limited to fifty percent of the first year premium and remains a level percentage in ensuing years. When a long-term care policy is replaced, the agent might be limited by law to a ten percent commission instead of the customary high commission on a new sale. Nevertheless, there is usually a financial incentive for the agent to replace the policy.

If you do switch policies, watch out for pre-existing conditions and other restrictions on coverage. Never drop your old policy until the new one is approved and effective. You should never buy more than one policy. Otherwise, you will be duplicating coverage, which is not a good idea.

The National Association of Insurance Commissioners (NAIC) has developed standards for marketing that have been adopted by many states and prohibit unethical sales practices. "Twisting" is one prohibited act, and occurs when the agent knowingly makes a misleading representation, or incomplete or fraudulent comparison of policies or insurers for the purpose of inducing a person to buy a different policy.

These standards also prohibit "high pressure tactics" and "cold lead advertising." The latter is the failure to conspicuously disclose that the purpose of the ad is to solicit insurance and that responding to the ad will result in being contacted by an agent or company. It is also completely improper for an insurance company or agent to send sales materials that appear as if they were sent by the Social Security Administration or some other government agency. In addition, the NAIC warns that consumers should not be misled by celebrity endorsements for long-term care policies.

Most states have a mandatory "free look" period on health insurance policies. The buyer has a period of time, sometimes thirty days, to review and return the policy without charge. Regardless of the length of the free look period, someone bullied or pressured into buying a policy may have a legal right to cancel the policy.

In most cases, you will have recourse against a pushy or abusive agent. You can file a complaint with your state's insurance department. Unfortunately, the state insurance department cannot recommend an agent. Usually it can only inform callers about complaints against a particular agent.

CHOOSING THE RIGHT AGENT

So how do you choose the right agent when you are in the market for a long-term care policy? *Parade* magazine reports that George Clooney once sold insurance for a living, so good looks could be reason enough for some people to choose one agent over another. Most agents, however, do not look like movie stars, so you had better have for a more substantial basis for your choice.

Looking through the phone book is another poor way to select an agent. The advertisements do not tell you much about the ethics of the person you are calling and they might describe only the types of products they sell.

Some radio stations have talk shows on which they discuss long-term care insurance. However, do not assume that the information you are getting is unbiased and impartial, or that the host has any special expertise on this subject. Often these programs are no more than infomercials. The host buys time from the radio station in the hope of selling lots of long-term care insurance policies.

In areas where there is a large elderly population, you will often see advertisements for free lunches at local hotels, sponsored by agents who are selling long-term care insurance. While these lunches are a good way to learn about long-term care policies, if you attend them they will also lead to sales calls. Nevertheless, if you have already decided you may want to purchase a policy, these luncheons can be a good way to see if the agent is someone with whom you would like to meet to discuss long-term care insurance.

If you are very happy with your current insurance agent, but he or she does not sell long-term care insurance, then you might ask your agent to recommend someone who does sell long-term care policies. Another hint is to look for someone who sells more than one long-term care policy. You should have a choice of policies and should not be limited to one particular company. An insurance broker who sells policies for many companies will know the advantages and disadvantages of each. If the broker is truly looking out for your interests, he or she will help you to analyze the positive and negative features of each policy.

Find an agent who is in business for the long term. You do not want someone who is selling insurance until a better job comes along. Look for someone who sells insurance for a living, rather than part-time. True insurance professionals know that it is in their best interest to sell the best product for the money, not the one that pays the highest commission.

In some states, the only requirement to sell insurance is the license application fee and a pulse. Other states have more stringent licensing requirements, along with continuing education requirements. It's not enough that your agent complies with the continuing education require-ments in your state. You should select an agent who has pursued designa-tions like the Chartered Life Underwriter (CLU) or the Chartered Financial Consultant (ChFC) awarded by the American College in Bryn Mawr, Pennsylvania. CLU and ChFC candidates must take insurance and financial planning courses. They must also meet ethical and experience requirements.

When you are ready to meet with an agent, call your state's insurance department. For one, the state agency can tell you if the agent is licensed to sell insurance. From time to time, you will hear horror stories about people pretending to be insurance agents who sell fake policies. The state insurance department may also be able to advise you if the agent has any complaints against him or her. The filing of complaints does not necessarily mean the agent did anything wrong, but it should make you cautious about dealing with that salesperson. As an additional precaution, you might call the company offering the policy to be certain that the individual is authorized to sell for it.

In January 1998, the California Department of Insurance became the first to offer access to agent and broker licensing information through the internet (*http://www.insurance.ca.gov*). Consumers can learn about disci-plinary actions taken against agents and brokers licensed in California. This information will include penalties invoked, as well as restriction, suspension or revocation of licenses. The Department also offers this information in a "Consumer Alert" publication.

Some industry groups are concerned that the due process rights of honest agents will be violated. They fear that agents might misuse the information to undercut a competitor.

As mentioned in Chapter 9, the Texas Insurance Department's Web site offers access to the Internet Complaints Information System. Consumers can learn a great deal about complaints against a particular agent. Depending upon the resources available to them, other state insurance departments may eventually offer similar services.

Ideally, you will find an agent who is genuinely concerned about finding a policy that meets your needs, and not a policy that pays the best commission for the agent.

Key Points: The Short Course on Long-Term Care Insurance

- *When selecting an agent or broker, look for one who possesses designations like the CLU or ChFC. Make sure the person is licensed to sell long-term care insurance in your state and has not been subjected to disciplinary action by the state's insurance department.*

- *Make certain the salesperson is interested in serving your needs and is not pushing the policy which pays the best commission. If the agent is too pushy and will not stop haranguing you to buy a policy, file a complaint with your state's insurance department. If an agent won't take "no" for an answer, advise him or her that you intend to file a complaint.*

- *Always keeps the agent's name and phone number with the policy. If you are incapacitated, this information should be readily available to whomever is acting upon your behalf.*

- *No matter how much you like the agent, always investigate the company that is issuing the policy. The best agent in the world will not be of much help if the company you are dealing with is not financially sound. On the other hand, a truly good agent will only deal with reputable insurance companies.*

- *Look for an agent who is a member of your community and has roots there. You should deal with salespeople who have a good reputation in the community and want to keep it. These salespeople know that word will travel fast if they do not look out for their clients.*

- *Watch out for the salesperson who makes features of the policy seem unique when they are really benefits that are required by law. For instance, the thirty-day "free look" period may be mandated by law in your state. The insurance company is not providing this feature out of the goodness of its heart. Another example is the reinstatement protection guaranteed by the Health Insurance Portability and Accountability Act of 1996, which protects policyholders who forget to pay their premium because of a cognitive impairment.*

Chapter 11

THE FINE PRINT

*W*e have discussed how to get the right price on a long-term care policy. No matter how little you pay, you have paid too much if the policy will not pay when you are in need of long-term care.

The old joke is that in the big print, insurance companies provide coverage, and in the small print, they take it away. Nonetheless, exclusions are not an evil conspiracy perpetrated by the insurance industry. If there were no exclusions, the insurance would not be affordable.

Even if you believe every word the salesperson says, always read the policy and the marketing materials. Pay particular attention to the exclusions in the policy. State law may require that all exclusions must be listed in the sales brochure. At a minimum, early in the sales process you should receive an Outline of Coverage that contains policy benefits and limitations.

Along with the Outline of Coverage, ask for a sample policy and look for the exclusions. If you decide to buy the policy, take advantage of the "free look" period and review it thoroughly. Make certain the exclusions are exactly the same as you believed and that the policy you bought is the same one that you reviewed previously.

Most exclusions are pretty innocuous. For example, no benefits are payable if your need for long-term care is the result of an act of war. Like many life insurance policies, there are also exclusions for suicide or attempted suicide. Alcoholism, drug addiction and mental retardation might also be excluded in a long-term care policy. A recent report indicated that alcoholism among the elderly is a significant problem.

Mental, psychoneurotic or personality disorders are often excluded. There should be no exclusion, however, for Alzheimer's disease and organic disorders. Organic disorders like Parkinson's disease are marked by an alteration in the brain's structure. Long-term care policies may also exclude losses that are payable under workers' compensation acts.

As one example, in Texas, policies may exclude coverage for conditions resulting from:

- Alcoholism and drug addiction;

- Illness caused by an act of war;

- Treatment already paid for by Medicare or any government program, except Medicaid;

- Attempted suicide or intentionally self-inflicted injuries;

- Service in the armed forces;

- Aviation activities, if you are not a fare-paying passenger; and

- Participation in a riot, felony or insurrection.

Still, you are not going to know all you need to know just by looking at the official list of exclusions in the long-term care policy. Insurance companies limit their obligation to pay throughout the policy. For example, they may only pay for care in certain kinds of facilities. Some will not pay for custodial care in a particular type of facility, even if the facility is licensed by the state to provide that kind of care. Furthermore, as mentioned earlier, long-term care insurers often restrict home health care payments and will not pay for care provided by a family member.

PRE-EXISTING CONDITIONS

Recently, I met a woman at a party who had tried to buy a long-term care policy for her husband ten years before, when she noticed he was becoming forgetful. The insurance company turned him down after interviewing him and seeing signs of memory loss. The man was diagnosed as suffering from the early stages of Alzheimer's disease and, knowing his condition would worsen, the insurer refused to write the policy. By the time I met her, the woman's husband had already spent nine years getting long-term care of some kind and was now in a nursing home.

There are certain medical problems you may have that will prevent you from being able to obtain long-term care insurance from some companies. Other companies may still write you a policy. Underwriting guidelines differ from company to company. While some long-term care insurers will cover diabetics, others will not. A woman with osteoporosis may be able to obtain a policy through one company, while she is rejected at another.

According to a survey of long-term care insurers conducted by StrateCision, Inc., a Massachusetts developer of software for agents, someone suffering from AIDS, cirrhosis, multiple sclerosis, muscular dystrophy, or Parkinson's disease will not be able to buy long-term care insurance. Other medical conditions like hypertension will put the applicant in a more expensive rating class, but won't necessarily lead to a rejection of the application for coverage.[1]

Exclusions are different from *pre-existing conditions*. A pre-existing condition is a medical problem for which you have received treatment or sought medical advice for prior to your applying for coverage. It is imperative that the applicant for coverage fully disclose all medical problems.

All companies look at the health of the applicant before selling a long-term care policy. Some insurers, however, use a process called "short-form" underwriting. There are only a few medical questions in this application, and if your answers are satisfactory the agent is authorized to issue you a policy on the spot. Other companies do a more thorough examination of your medical history and are much more selective about who they will insure.

Some companies utilize a practice called *post-claims underwriting*, which is illegal in some states. These companies do not investigate your medical history *until* you file a claim. However, at that time, they may attempt to deny you benefits if there are any inconsistencies between your application and your medical history. A company that thoroughly investigates your medical history before issuing a policy is less likely to practice this kind of claims denial. The National Association of Insurance Commissioners is working on a model regulation that will prohibit post-claims underwriting.

If you have health problems, a company may still issue a policy. However, those health problems often will not be covered by the policy for a specified period of time. Health problems like this are viewed as pre-existing conditions, since they were present prior to the inception of the policy. For example, if you suffer from certain types of cancer, the company may issue a policy that is subject to a six month wait for coverage of the pre-existing conditions.

Usually you must wait six months before pre-existing conditions are covered, although this time varies from company to company. In addition, each state has different rules regarding pre-existing conditions. If you are buying a tax-qualified policy, the pre-existing condition must be covered after no later than six months from the inception of the policy.

In Wisconsin, once a person is insured and has satisfied any waiting period, the long-term care insurer may not refuse benefits for irreversible dementia such as Alzheimer's disease, provided the person needs the care covered by the policy. Therefore, a long-term care insurer could not deny coverage to someone with Alzheimer's disease by saying it was a pre-existing condition. Because an Alzheimer's patient might need care for many years, an unethical insurer may be tempted to try to deny coverage on this basis.

To avoid problems down the road, some states require full *front-end underwriting* before the purchase, unless it is a guaranteed-issue policy. The insurer is required to thoroughly investigate your medical history before issuing the policy. Unlike short-form underwriting, this lets the purchaser avoid encountering pre-existing condition problems later on. In either case, making misrepresentations or failing to disclose pertinent medical information can cause the policy to be voided.

Texas also has something akin to an *incontestability clause*. This clause states that once your policy has been in effect for two years, a company cannot cancel it or refuse to pay a claim because of misstatements in the application. Nevertheless, if it is decided that there was an intent on your part to deceive or fraud, then you may still have difficulty receiving your benefits, even after two years.

Avoid any agent who encourages you to shade the truth on an application for long-term care insurance coverage, or who glosses over the fine print in a policy. These kinds of agents are worried more about their commission than they are about your having coverage when you need it.

Key Points: The Short Course on Long-Term Care Insurance

- *Look for any language in the policy that limits or restricts your right to collect benefits. This language will not necessarily be found in the policy exclusions. Make sure you get an Outline of Coverage early in the sales process. Take advantage of the "free look" period and thoroughly review any policy you have bought.*

- *Always fully disclose your medical problems on the application. Otherwise, the insurer may have a basis for challenging your claim later. See if the long-term care policy has any language which would keep the company from making this challenge after a specific length of time.*

- *Look for language in the policy related to pre-existing conditions. A pre-existing condition should be covered after no longer than six months.*

- *Watch carefully for exclusions relating to Alzheimer's disease and organic brain disorders. These conditions should be fully covered by any long-term care policy you buy.*

- *A policy might contain an age restriction related to its purchase. You might be too young or too old to qualify for a policy.*

Chapter 12

GROUP LONG-TERM
CARE INSURANCE

*F*or some people, the following schedule describes a typical week in their life. They put in sixty hours at the office. If they are lucky, they make it to the day care center before it closes at 7:00 p.m. Over the weekend, they will be helping aging parents with chores around the house, so Mom and Dad will not try to do the work themselves. These overworked individuals will also be using the weekend to catch up on work around their own house.

They know the situation may worsen as their parents age. Although their parents struggle to be independent, they are losing a step or two each year. At some point, Mom and Dad may need more than just help around the house. The time may come when they need long-term care on a full-time basis.

If your week is anything like this scenario, your employer may have a solution that is more than just one family care day a year. Just as many people rely on their employer for health insurance, group long-term care policies may also be available at some places of business. Companies have come to realize that employees will be more productive if they do not bear the burden of providing long-term care to a parent or spouse. Nearly one in four U.S. households (i.e., 22.4 million) is involved in caring for a person age 50 or older.[1]

Group long-term care policies are a relatively new benefit few employers offer. According to the American Council of Life Insurance, employer-sponsored plans now constitute 12 percent of the long-term care insurance market. A total of 1260 employers offer group coverage, up from two in 1987.[2] According to the Health Insurance Association of America, that number grew to 1,532 in 1996, a 21.6 percent increase. With that increase, group plans now account for almost 20 percent of all long-term care policy sales. Because of changes in the law, group long-term care insurance is likely to become a more popular employee benefit.

The Health Insurance Portability and Accountability Act of 1996 created a tax break for employers who pay long-term care policy premiums on behalf of their employees. Employers may deduct these premiums as a business expense, just as they are able to deduct health insurance payments they make on an employee's behalf. Even though the employer may deduct those premiums, the money paid on the employee's behalf is not treated as income to the worker; that is, the money the company pays on the employee's behalf will not show up in the worker's W-2 form.

According to Janice Stanger, Ph.D., a consultant in the San Francisco actuarial consulting firm of William M. Mercer, Inc., enrollees in group long-term care plans pay the full cost as a general rule.[3] And, unlike traditional health insurance policies, the employer usually does not contribute to the cost of the coverage. Nevertheless, because the underwriting base consists of younger members, the premium is likely to be lower for enrollees. Furthermore, because marketing expenses are lower, a "group rate" will apply and the premium will usually be twenty to thirty percent cheaper.

In a group plan, the underwriting base is more favorable. The plan will attract a wide variety of participants, not just individuals who feel they will need long-term care in the near future. According to the American Council of Life Insurance, the average age of people buying policies is 63 years. The average age of insureds who are buying employer-sponsored plans is 43 years.[2]

In addition to the favorable underwriting base, insureds do not have to worry about finding a reputable agent. The employer's benefits department usually negotiates with the long-term care insurer. The risk of fraud or of overreaching is, therefore, considerably less.

Some group plans may even allow the employees' family members, including parents and in-laws, to buy long-term care insurance through the company at the group rate. Retired employees might also be eligible for the long-term care insurance plan. According to Stanger, children are typically not covered by the group policy.

Group plans may not require a physical exam. Therefore, someone who has health problems may still qualify for coverage. Some policies that are offered on a guaranteed-issue basis will require proof of insurability for retirees and parents, as well as in-laws. These policies cannot be canceled unless premiums are not paid or if the maximum benefit is exhausted.

Group long-term care policies are also portable, which means that employees covered under a group policy may continue their coverage even if they leave their place of employment. Normally, if the group plan is discontinued and you have been covered for more than six months, you may convert to an individual policy. To convert to an individual policy at this point, you would not need to provide evidence of insurability.

Sometimes, organizations to which you belong (such as a union) will offer group long-term care policies. You cannot assume that an organization you trust will offer a wonderful long-term care policy. These policies must still be examined carefully to determine the quality of the coverage.

KEEP YOUR GUARD UP

Whether it is your employer or another group offering the policy, ask questions before signing up. The numbers may not add up. For example, a self-funded, group long-term care policy that offers modest premiums for a $120 maximum daily nursing home benefit and a $250,000 maximum benefit may seem attractive, until you read that there is an $1800 per month ceiling on the benefit. Until you see the cap on benefits, you might think you will get $120 per day and $3600 in a thirty-day month. The $1800 will not come close to covering a month in a nursing home.

Even if your employer does not offer group long-term care insurance, the company may offer other benefits that will help. Many companies offer Employee Assistance Programs (EAP). EAP counselors may advise employees regarding services that are available to the person in need of long-term care. By calling the EAP counselors, you might be pointed in the right direction or at least you will find a sympathetic ear.

Do not forget about the Family and Medical Leave Act of 1993. Under this law, you may be entitled to unpaid leave to care for a family member who is incapable of participating in his or her regular daily activities.

In addition, there may be other state or local laws that permit leaves of absence to provide care for a relative. It is also possible that your employer has its own policy regarding time off to care for family members. Check your employee handbook or manual.

Finally, take some time out of your busy schedule to discuss issues of long-term care with your parents and family members. The best time to discuss and plan for the risk of needing long-term care is *before* you or a loved one need it.

Key Points: The Short Course on Long-Term Care Insurance

- *Group policies through your employer should offer a more reasonable premium, because the underwriting base consists of a mix of older and younger individuals. Also, there are less marketing expenses associated with these policies. In addition, the contract is usually negotiated by a knowledgeable person at your company who should be in a position to secure the best coverage for the money.*

- *Group long-term care policies through an employer make coverage accessible to employees. Workers are able to pay for the coverage through payroll deduction, which makes the premium less painful.*

- *Group long-term care policies make sense for the employer, because they increase employee productivity and loyalty.*

- *Yet you must still "do the math" with any group long-term care policy you are considering. The daily and lifetime benefit may be sufficient, but the monthly cap might be inadequate.*

Chapter 13

COVERAGE FOR HOME HEALTH CARE

*O*ne woman wrote a letter published in Ann Landers' column after reading numerous letters from wives who complained about their husbands being underfoot. The reader said that her husband was diagnosed with Lou Gehrig's disease at age 56. Within 18 months, he became a quadriplegic and was on a ventilator. The woman cared for him at home for six years until his death.[1]

This woman's point was that she would have loved to have her husband follow her around the kitchen, getting in her way. She advised other women to count their blessings and to stop complaining.

Caring for someone at home is no easy task. This woman did it for six years. Her husband was relatively young. Unfortunately, the situation is not an isolated one. Women frequently find themselves as caregivers for parents, a husband and sometimes for both. Members of the "sandwich generation" may find themselves caring for parents while they are still raising their own children. The average woman can expect to spend 17 years caring for a child and 18 years caring for an elderly parent.[2]

The home health care industry is growing due to the need for caregivers. In the world of television, the caregiver on the sitcom "Frasier" is the lovable home health aide, Daphne Moon. Daphne lives in the house and takes care of Frasier Crane's father, Martin.

But television is not real life. Whereas home health care can be blessing for many people, there are problems within the industry. In Florida, one home health aide was accused of stealing thousands of dollars from at least eleven senior citizens. The aide wrote $17,000 worth of fraudulent checks off the account of one of the people for whom she was providing care.[3]

In one "Dear Abby" advice column, the neighbor of a man who died warned other readers about "caregivers" who take advantage of the elderly. The man was starved and neglected by his live-in caregiver. The caregiver induced the man to change his will and took seven to ten vacations a year, leaving him without care during her absences.[4]

Florida requires home health care aides to undergo a criminal background check, along with a screening that is given by the Department of Children and Families. Unfortunately, the home health care agency may rely upon documents that have been provided by the very person it is hiring to perform home health care services.

In choosing a home health care agency, ask for references from the provider and call a few of those references yourself. Make certain the agency does a background check on the person coming into your home and does not rely on documentation supplied by the aide. Ask how long the person has worked for the agency. Call the branch of state government that regulates home health care in your state to see if it has a record of complaints about a particular agency. If it is Medicare certified, ask to see the Medicare Survey Report, which is a quality control mechanism.

WHAT IS HOME HEALTH CARE?

Throughout this book, it has been assumed that most people would like to spend their last days in the comfort of their home. Home health care makes that possible for many people.

Home health care is defined as medical and nonmedical services, provided to ill, disabled or infirm persons in their residences. The home health care category covers skilled nursing care as well as other services such as therapy or assistance with the activities of daily living.

Home health care describes a variety of services. One company advertises that it can provide the "solution to your home health care needs." Their services include:

- Personal care needs on an hourly or daily basis;
- Alzheimer's disease and dementia care;

- Home health aides;
- Homemaker services; and
- Live-in care.

The company describes itself as licensed, responsible, qualified, caring, friendly, insured and bonded.

All too often, people cannot afford to pay a company for home health care services. Family members often provide nonmedical services for a loved one, but some policies will not pay for this. According to the Health Insurance Association of America, bringing an aide into your home just three times a week can easily cost $12,000 per year.[5]

INSURANCE COVERAGE FOR HOME HEALTH CARE

According to an economics professor at the University of Maryland's Center on Aging, at one time long-term care insurers were reluctant to cover home health care. Now it is difficult to sell a policy which does not contain coverage for home health care.

Typically, new insurance policies are developed to address needs that are not being met by existing policies. For example, there is limited coverage for home health care under the typical health insurance policy. Most health insurance policies will not pay for homemaker services, cus-todial care or home-delivered meals. If the need for long-term care results from a car accident, there may be coverage under an auto insurance policy.

Medicare's coverage for home health care is limited to care that is restorative in nature. As a general rule, it will not pay for nonmedical services such as meals delivered to the home. Nor will Medicare pay for homemaker services such as shopping, cleaning and laundry.

Medicare will not pay for home health care that is custodial, unless it is related to treatment of an illness or injury and is accompanied by skilled nursing care or therapy. Medicare considers personal care to be custodial in nature and therefore will not pay for care provided by home health aides such as bathing, toileting or helping the patient get dressed.

Medicare will pay for most hospice care in the United States, but that is for people who have less than six months to live. As a general rule, to qualify for hospice care, a Medicare beneficiary must be covered under Part

A for hospitalization. In addition, the beneficiary's doctor as well as the hospice director must certify that he or she has less than six months to live. An additional requirement is that the beneficiary must agree not to seek curative treatment for the terminal illness and must waive the standard Medicare coverage for the medical problem.

And to repeat a point made earlier, although Medicare supplemental policies plug many of the gaps in Medicare coverage, home health care still slips through the cracks. Medigap policies rarely pay for home health care.

Until recently, Medicaid paid only for care in a nursing home. Now, there are programs in some areas where Medicaid will pay for home health care. Many people turn to Medicaid when they run out of funds to pay for long-term care.

HOME HEALTH CARE AND THE LONG-TERM CARE POLICY

A long-term care policy is not worth buying unless it includes coverage for home health care. Some companies will offer coverage for home health care as a stand-alone policy. Obviously, that is not as good as buying a comprehensive long-term care policy, but it is better than having no policy at all.

One major insurer's home care-only policy which may be considered "typical" covers the following:

- Skilled care
- Adult day care
- Hospice care
- Home health aide services
- Personal care services
- Homemaker services
- Therapeutic services
- Caregiver training
- Medical alert device.

Home health care coverage may also be sold as part of a comprehensive long-term care policy. Make certain that the insurance company's use of the term "comprehensive" is clear. One major long-term care insurer uses "comprehensive" to describe its long-term care insurance plan, but the policy requires a rider to obtain home and community-based care coverage. On the bright side, by purchasing the rider, no prior hospital stay is required as a prerequisite to receiving home and community-based care.

The home health care benefit in a long-term care insurance policy is usually a specified percentage of the nursing home coverage. Most often, it is fifty percent of the nursing home benefit. Consequently, a policy with a $200 per day benefit would normally contain a $100 daily benefit for home health care.

A good home health care policy should provide homemaker and companion services. The services include housekeeping, laundry, grocery shopping, cleaning, cooking, and bill paying. Some policies will allow friends, neighbors and relatives to perform homemaker services, as long as they do not live in the same house as the person insured.

A 79-year-old man purchased a stand-alone home health care policy, which also offered homemaker and companion benefits. He bought a two-year benefit of $100 per day, and paid $1900 per year.

Some policies offer discounts on services provided by home health care agencies. The discounts apply even if your policy does not cover the service. You are not obligated to use any particular provider.

COMMUNITY CARE BENEFITS

Chapter 3 described different settings of care. Most people want to be cared for in their own home if they can no longer care for themselves. If that is no longer possible, many of us would prefer care that bridges the gap between our house and the dreaded nursing home.

Community care is an option for people who are looking for a "middle ground." As the name suggests, community care helps you function effectively, while maintaining your place in the general community. Community care encompasses home health care, as well as other services. Community care would include assisted living facilities, adult day care, adult day health care, board-and-care homes, adult congregate living, and continuing care retirement communities.

According to Samuel X. Kaplan, founder of U.S. Care in Santa Monica, California, only a handful of long-term care insurers have introduced policies that include coverage for community care services. Many policies offer adult day care as a benefit but most do not offer the full gamut of community care benefit options from which customers can pick and choose. Kaplan, whose company designs, develops and implements long-term care products, contends that expanding community care benefits will reduce claim costs. The average cost per day for a private room in an assisted living facility is $71.6

In his pitch to sell long-term care insurance, one agent recommended upgrading a home health care plan into one that covers assisted living, as well as personal care facilities, Alzheimer centers, and adult congregate living facilities. The newer plans offer broader coverage, according to the agent. Whereas it generally does not pay to switch one policy for another, these additional benefits may be worth adding. As always, however, be wary of pre-existing condition problems and the cost of buying a new policy when you are older.

As more long-term care insurers add community care benefits, there will be more options for consumers. Chapter 2 described some of the many housing and living arrangements that are available for seniors. If a policy offers community care benefits, it means that there may be some coverage available for assisted living residences. Naturally, you will still have to meet the eligibility standard that exists in every long-term care policy.

Most of us want to spend our final days in a comfortable and familiar environment, surrounded by family, friends and loved ones. Home health care coverage can make that final wish possible.

Key Points: The Short Course on Long-Term Care Insurance

- *A home health care policy does not fully cover you against the risk of needing long-term care. Nevertheless, if you want to stay in your home for as long as possible, the policy can provide financial resources to make that possible.*

- *Make sure a hospital or nursing home stay is not a prerequisite to receiving home health care benefits.*

- *The home health care benefit in a long-term care policy is usually fifty percent of the nursing home benefit.*

- *Community care benefits amount to much more than adult day care. A few policies will pay for assisted living and personal care facilities. An assisted living benefit can sometimes be added to a home care or nursing home policy.*

Chapter 14

ALTERNATIVES TO LONG-TERM CARE POLICIES

*I*ndividual long-term care policies are quite expensive and may be out of your price range. In addition, group long-term care policies may not be available to you. The question remains as to how you can plan for the risk that you may need long-term care.

Practicing risk management as a means of reducing the likelihood of needing long-term care was discussed earlier in this book. That is, you try to plan for the day when long-term care is necessary. In the right house and with the right help coming in, you just might be able to live out your days in your own home, which is the dream of many people.

You may be able to use some of the insurance products you already own to finance long-term care if it should become necessary. For example, many life insurance products now include an "accelerated death benefit." The policyholder can tap into the death benefit to finance long-term care or to meet the expenses of a catastrophic illness. If the policy conditions are satisfied, he or she can draw upon the death benefit.

The policy pays out a percentage of the death benefit early if long-term care is needed. With some policies, the insured collects a percentage of the death benefit each month up to a maximum of 100 percent. Some policies make payment in a lump sum. In essence, you are taking an advance payment of the death benefit. The accelerated death benefit is sometimes called a *living benefit*.

The triggering mechanism for this benefit will vary from policy to policy. Needing home health care may be enough justification to tap the policy. Other policies may require confinement to a nursing home or to an assisted living facility, due to inability to perform the "activities of daily living."

Accelerated death benefit riders are a relatively new product. Some companies offer the option at no additional premium, but may impose an interest charge on the amount advanced if the benefit is used. In any event, these riders should not be confused with borrowing against a policy's cash value. The accelerated death benefit is not dependent upon the policy's cash value. It's a percentage of the policy's face value. For example, a policy with a $100,000 death benefit might have little or no cash value. These riders are also available on term life policies which have no cash value.

These living benefit riders have become very popular. Nevertheless, they are not an adequate substitute for long-term care insurance, because the amount advanced will not necessarily pay for the needed long-term care. Furthermore, there is a danger that tapping the death benefit will leave insufficient life insurance for beneficiaries of the policy.

The marketing materials for one insurance company tout the dual nature of its universal life insurance policy. You can use the policy to pay for qualified long-term care expenses, and any portion of the death benefit not used will be paid out when you die. This particular product pays up to 100 percent of the daily costs for qualified long-term care services up to a monthly maximum of two percent of the face value of the policy. The amount paid out for long-term care will be deducted from the death benefit. There is a ninety day elimination period, so you will have to wait about three months to collect. To qualify, the insured must be chronically ill. He or she must be unable to perform without substantial assistance at least two of the ADLs for a period of at least ninety days. The other qualifying language requires that the individual needs substantial supervision to protect him or her from threats to health and safety due to severe cognitive impairment.

Make certain you are not causing yourself a tax problem by taking an advance on your life insurance to pay for long-term care. Normally, when the death benefit is accelerated to pay for long-term care expenses, you will not run into a tax problem; however, you should check with an accountant. It is also important to know that receiving these advances from your life insurance policy may affect you and your family's eligibility for Medicaid.

Life insurance policies are not unique in offering this benefit to pay for long-term care. A similar approach is now being utilized to a limited extent with annuities and disability insurance. A few companies are offering annuities and disability policies with long-term care riders.

VIATICAL SETTLEMENTS

Accelerated death benefits from a life insurance policy should not be confused with *viatical settlements*. With a viatical settlement, the life insurance policy of a terminally-ill individual is sold for cash to an investor for a percentage of its face value. The investor collects on the policy when the individual dies.

In certain areas of the country, you can see advertisements for investors that promise a great rate of return and absolute safety. The money invested is used to buy the policies of people who are terminally ill.

The viatical settlement industry is growing. While the premise seems distasteful, proponents argue that the individuals selling policies need cash to make their final days more comfortable. These individuals need money to pay their expenses, such as rent and medicine. A life insurance policy will not do them much good after they are gone. Nevertheless, it is disturbing to see advertisements which suggest that your rate of return will be 42 percent after 36 months.

The people marketing viatical settlements argue that they are permitting terminally ill patients to "choose how to live the last months of life." Of course, in the same sales pitch, one marketer assures investors that three different physicians are used to verify the patient's medical status. The inference is that investors do not need to worry that the patient will get well.

A *Wall Street Journal* article written by Lynn Asinof suggests there are risks to selling your life insurance policy. New drugs and medical advances have given people who are diagnosed with major illnesses a second chance. If these individuals have sold their life insurance policies and have raided their retirement accounts, thinking the end was near, they may not have enough money to live on should they be cured.[1]

A similar problem might face individuals who sell their assets to pay for long-term care or who take advances on their life insurance policies. If they recover or linger on longer than expected, their financial problems will mount. More than likely, they will have to fall back upon a government program like Medicaid.

Many states are considering whether to regulate the viatical settlement industry. Twenty-five states have no viatical laws whatsoever. When regulations are enacted, the state insurance department is usually given authority to sanction companies that don't play by the rules.[2]

OTHER POSSIBILITIES

The beginning of this book mentioned the practice of self-insuring against the risk of needing long-term care. The strategy is to put money aside and invest it for the day when long-term care might become necessary. With the cost of long-term care escalating rapidly, you would need to build up a huge account to pay those expenses, if and when that event occurs.

One possibility is to invest the premiums you would pay to a long-term care insurer yourself. The problem is that not everyone has the discipline to save on a regular basis. Whereas those same individuals will pay their insurance bill when it arrives in the mail, they do not have the discipline to invest the same amount. Even if they do save money on a regular basis, they are likely to raid the account for some reason other than needing long-term care.

Consumer Reports suggests that if you put away roughly $160,000, you may not need to buy a long-term care policy.[3] The rationale is that if you put aside that much money, you will have enough to pay for roughly four years in a nursing home at an average cost of $40,000 per year. You will have sufficient resources to pay for a lengthy nursing home stay, as long as the return on your investment keeps up with the expected increases in the cost of long-term care. Even if you do save your premiums and invest them well, your nest-egg may not be nearly enough to cover the cost of long-term care.

Key Points: The Short Course on Long-Term Care Insurance

- *With the accelerated death benefit rider, you may be entitled to collect all or part of your death benefit from the insurer if you need long-term care or have some catastrophic illness. With a viatical settlement, a dying person sells his or her life insurance policy to investors for a percentage of its face value.*

- *While there are alternatives to long-term care insurance such as life insurance policies that advance the death benefit, the best way to insure against the risk of needing long-term care is with a long-term care policy. By doing so, you have purchased the appropriate policy to cover that risk. Otherwise, you are buying incidental coverage for long-term care if it becomes necessary.*

- *If you do buy a policy to protect against both risks, make certain you are not overpaying for the privilege. Shop around for the best price on long-term care insurance, as well as for life insurance policies. You may do better by buying the policies separately. And if you do not need life insurance, do not buy a policy just because it includes coverage for long-term care.*

- *If you have sufficient resources and are not worried about preserving assets for your heirs, consider self-insuring against the risk of needing long-term care. If you view the risk as too great to take, buy a long-term care policy with a longer elimination period.*

Chapter 15

SEPARATING THE TRUTH FROM THE HYPE

*T*hroughout this book, we have looked at some of the advantages and disadvantages associated with long-term care insurance. Whether or not to purchase a policy is a very personal decision. There are many compelling arguments for buying a policy. On the other hand, not everyone needs a policy. You should be aware that while some insurance agents make a genuine effort to educate you on how to buy the best policy that will meet your needs, others will try anything to convince you to buy a long-term care policy. Unfortunately, too many insurance agents are worried more about their need for another commission than they are about selling you a policy that meets your needs. Chapter 10 provided some advice on how you might protect yourself from these agents. It might also help to look at the different sales pitches that may come your way and learn to recognize the truth from the hype.

Pitch: You should buy a long-term care policy because it is a write-off.

Truth: While that may be true, many people who buy a long-term care insurance policy will not be able to take advantage of the tax write-off. First of all, you must itemize deductions before you are able to include premiums paid on a qualified long-term care insurance policy. Many buyers of long-term care policies are older and no longer itemize deductions on their tax return. Often, they take the standard deduction, so the tax write-off means nothing.

Even if you itemize your deductions, the deduction for medical and dental expenses is limited. You can only deduct the amount of your medical and dental expenses that is more than 7.5 percent of your adjusted gross income. Therefore, if your adjusted gross income is $50,000, your non-reimbursed medical and dental expenses must be greater than $3,750 before the premium for a long-term care policy does you any good.

If you are paying $4,000 a year or more for a long-term care policy, it might appear at first that you are going to exceed the cap right away and get some sort of deduction. The problem is that you are not able to include the full premium of a qualified long-term care policy in your deduction for medical and dental expenses. If you are 51 to 60, you can only include $770 in calculating your deduction. If you are 61 to 70, the limit on your deductible medical expense is $2,050.

Therefore, if your adjusted gross income is $50,000, you are still far short of having a tax deduction, no matter what you pay in premiums. Even with a $2,050 expense for buying a long-term care policy, it will not make any difference in your taxes. It will not mean anything until you exceed the $3,750 (i.e., 7.5 percent of your gross income) threshold for taking a deduction.

Even if a tax-qualified policy will help your tax situation, do not assume you must buy a new policy to get the deduction. The premium on your current policy, if you have one, may be deductible. As a general rule, policies sold prior to January 1, 1997 will receive favorable tax treatment.

Pitch: The state insurance department approved this policy.

Truth: Another pitch is to imply that the state insurance department endorses a particular long-term care policy. The salesperson will say that it is approved by the department. Although the policy may be approved for sale, that does not mean it is therefore a good one to purchase. State approval only means the policy has met the minimum standards required by law.

The salesperson might also boast that the policy has a "free look" period. However, this benefit is often guaranteed by law and is not a particular perk of this policy. Most states have a mandatory "free look" period on health insurance policies. The buyer always has a period of time, often thirty days, to review and return the policy without charge.

Every state has safeguards in place to protect people who buy insurance. Certain coverage are mandated by law. Before you buy a long-term care policy, find out what features the policy must contain. By doing so, you will ensure that a salesperson will not tout as unique a particular feature that is contained in every policy sold in your state. Ask your insurance department for a brochure which explains the specific policy requirements in your state.

Pitch: If you keep the policy you have now, you're going to be really sorry someday.

Truth: You should question any agent who is attempting to get you to replace your current policy. Sometimes agents will try to sell you a policy to replace the one they sold you years ago. They will assure you that this new and improved policy is much better. However, before you purchase a new policy, recognize that your current policy may be more than adequate and that there are risks associated with replacing it. Furthermore, since the premium is usually based upon your age at the time of purchase, you will be in a more expensive rate class.

Sometimes, the policy you currently have may be upgraded for a minimal amount, rather than buying a new policy. The agent makes a much better commission, however, by replacing it. Part of the pitch is to bad-mouth the other policies that are on the market. When an agent has nothing good to say about his competitor's policy, you should question the ethics of the salesperson.

"Twisting" is a practice that is specifically prohibited by law. This is when the agent knowingly makes a misleading representation or incomplete or fraudulent comparison of policies or insurers for the purpose of inducing a person to buy a different policy.

Many times, if an agent represents more than one company, the danger is that instead of recommending the best policy for you, the agent will choose the one that pays him or her the best commission. Some companies will promise agents higher commissions or bonuses for selling a certain number of policies, and many insurance companies offer trips and other incentives for selling their products. The best agents will give you the pros and cons of each long-term care policy they offer.

With all that said, buying a new, tax-qualified policy will assure you that it meets certain standards, such as the benefits eligibility trigger. Newer policies may also offer community care benefits, such as coverage for assisted living.

Pitch: If you buy now, you will lock in the price forever.

Truth: For most policies, the price you pay is based upon your age when you buy the policy. Only an unethical agent will assure you that the premium will never go up. The agent should inform you that the premium may go up if state insurance regulators grant a rate increase for everyone in your rate classification.

Because long-term care insurance is a relatively new product, insurers do not have sufficient underwriting data to predict the number of claims that may come at a later date. Long-term care policies have what is known as a "long tail," which means that the claims may not be filed for many years.

When the price of a policy does go up, the buyer is left in a difficult position. Since the premium is based upon age at the time of purchase, the insured cannot just switch companies, for the premium will increase considerably. Furthermore, the insured may not be healthy enough to qualify for a policy at a different company.

Pitch: Don't worry about the financial rating of the company, because there is a state guaranty fund that insures your policy.

Truth: On the contrary, it is very important to find out the financial rating of the company backing the long-term care policy. A.M. Best, Standard & Poor, Duff & Phelps, Moody's and Weiss all are good rating agencies. If a company has received a rating below A+ from A.M. Best, avoid it, unless you are having trouble finding a company to insure you.

Some salespeople will tell you that because there is a guaranty fund in your state, you do not need to be concerned about the financial health of the carrier. Guaranty funds should give you a feeling of security, but they are not the equivalent of the F.D.I.C. insurance on your bank account. If the company that sold you a long-term care policy experiences financial problems, it can mean a lot of trouble for you. Since it may be decades until you need the policy, stay away from a company that has not been around for decades already.

The hardest pitch to deal with is the high-pressure tactics used by an unethical agent, the agent who insists that you buy the policy immediately or you will lose out on some special benefit. No one should buy a long-term care policy without reading it carefully and reviewing it with a trusted advisor. Do not sign anything until you have investigated the agent and the company offering the policy. High pressure sales tactics are illegal. You should pitch any agent who uses them right out of your home.

Key Points: The Short Course on Long-Term Care Insurance

- *The fact that part of your long-term care premium is deductible should not be the reason you are buying a policy. Only a portion of the premium is used to calculate your deduction. Even with the write-off for long-term care premiums, many people do not exceed the 7.5 percent of their adjusted gross income which is the point at which the deduction will do them any good.*

- *State insurance laws determine what minimum coverage should be included in every policy sold in your state. If you buy a tax-qualified policy, it will contain certain provisions mandated by the Health Insurance Portability and Accountability Act of 1996.*

- *Replacing the long-term care policy you have now is always good for the agent, because it means a new commission and possible sales bonuses. It will not necessarily result in a better policy for you, however. In fact, it may even raise a pre-existing condition problem for you. Also, if you buy a new policy, you will be in a new rate class because of your increased age.*

- *You can never lock in the price of a long-term care policy forever. The premium may be raised if state regulators approve a price increase for everyone in your rate class.*

- *You always need to worry about the financial rating of the company that issues a long-term care policy you're considering. The backing of the guaranty fund in your state will not necessarily protect you, should the long-term care insurer experience financial setbacks.*

Chapter 16

WHERE TO GO FOR HELP

A commercial for Hallmark greeting cards shows a young woman watching from her window as her elderly neighbor goes to the mailbox day after day, only to find it empty. The older woman returns to her house looking very despondent. Since it is a commercial for Hallmark, you might have guessed by now that the young woman buys her elderly neighbor a greeting card and sends her young son to deliver it. The card cheers up the older woman, and she gives the younger one a hug.

While it is an effective commercial, real life problems are not fixed so easily. A greeting card will not solve the problems of the elderly. Nevertheless, more of these random acts of kindness certainly cannot hurt. Having supportive neighbors will help the elderly remain in their homes for a lot longer.

When you or a loved one needs long-term care, you will face many psychological and financial issues. Perhaps you live thousands of miles away from a parent who suddenly or gradually requires long-term care. Even if your parent has long-term care insurance, problems will arise that are difficult to resolve, especially when you live so far away.

Sometimes an immediate problem is dealing with the sadness, guilt, anger and helplessness that you may experience when a loved one requires care. To help cope with these feelings, you might begin with a call to the Employee Assistance Program, if one is available through your employer. Oftentimes these programs provide access to a counselor who may be able to help you deal with the emotions you are experiencing. EAP counselors are also aware of local social service programs that might be available to assist the person in need of long-term care.

FAMILY AND MEDICAL LEAVE

The Family and Medical Leave Act of 1993 (FMLA) may be a godsend if you need to make arrangements for the person in need of long-term care. One woman in Coral Springs, Florida, took advantage of the Act to search for the right nursing home for her mother. In the end, she brought her mother to live with her.

However, FMLA does not apply to every employee at every company. You must have worked at least 1,250 hours in the 12 months preceding a leave. If eligible, you qualify for unpaid, short-term family and medical leave of up to 12 weeks in any 12 month period. The "unpaid" part is what discourages many people who genuinely need to take a leave but cannot afford to. At a time when they may be facing additional expenses to pay for the long-term care of a relative, few can manage to take time off without pay.

The circumstances that warrant a leave are specific. An employee may be granted leave to care for a spouse, son, daughter, or parent with a serious health condition requiring medical treatment that renders that family member incapable of participating in his or her regular daily activities. According to an article originally appearing in *The Wall Street Journal*, interest in family leave has risen, partly because of growing eldercare needs. However, the same article reported that some employers deny leaves, fail to reinstate leave-takers to the same job, or retaliate against them in some way.[1] If this were to happen, the employee's recourse is to file a complaint with the Department of Labor or to take legal action.

WHERE TO FIND HELP IF YOU DON'T LIVE NEARBY

A dentist in upstate New York found himself in a difficult dilemma. His mother had died several years earlier, and now his father, who lived in Florida, was slipping away. Neighbors of his father would call the dentist to report that his dad was not eating or taking care of himself. Because of his busy dental practice, the man found it extremely difficult to leave.

Frustrated, he attempted to resolve the problem from over a thousand miles away. The problem persisted for years.

Initially, the dentist was able to find his father an assisted living residence. For a time, his father seemed to do better. The staff of the assisted living facility made sure his elderly father came down to the eating area for meals and took his medicine. Periodically, however, the dentist received a call regarding his father's failing health. Finally it was clear that the older man was becoming too ill to stay at the assisted living residence.

The dentist was forced to deal with finding a nursing home for his father. Eventually he found a facility that cost almost $5,000 per month. Along with the fixed monthly charge, the cost of a nutritional supplement was added to the bill. The father's limited assets were gradually eaten away by the expense.

Even though the nursing home was reputed to be a good one, there were questions about the care his father was receiving. Relatives in the area would drop in occasionally and find that the nursing home resident was seemingly unattended. His hair had not been cut in months and he was unshaven. After numerous calls to the facility, the administrator promised that the elderly man would receive better care.

The dentist's father lived in that nursing home for nearly two years. Throughout the last years of his father's life, the dentist agonized over whether he was doing the right thing. He always felt torn between his work responsibilities and the obligation he owed to his father.

Along with finding care for his father, the dentist dealt with dozens of other problems. He had to sell his father's condominium and handle his administrative affairs. In addition, health care, insurance, and legal issues cropped up constantly.

What do you do when you are thousands of miles away from someone you love who is in need of long-term care? It is hard enough when you live in the same city. Resolving these problems from a distance can be a nightmare.

FIRST STOP: THE ELDERCARE LOCATOR

The Eldercare Locator is a public service sponsored by the Administration on Aging, U.S. Department of Health and Human Services. It is administered by the National Association of Area Agencies on Aging and the National Association of State Units on Aging. By calling (800) 677-1116, you can locate local support resources for aging Americans. It can put people in touch with state and local services that enable individuals to remain independent in their own homes.

Creation of these Area Agencies on Aging came about as a result of the Older Americans Act of 1965. In Florida, the role of the Area Agencies on Aging is to administer programs for older Americans, such as Emergency Home Energy Assistance for the Elderly. It also administers the Community Care for the Elderly, the Alzheimer's Disease Initiative, and the Home Care for the Elderly programs.

The Eldercare Locator brochure lists some typical questions from Eldercare Locator callers. For example:

- Our uncle just died and my aunt lives two hundred miles away. Is there a service available that can look in on her and do some household chores?

- My grandmother is complaining about the care in her nursing home. Can you suggest someone to contact to check on the situation?

- Our neighbor has no family. Is there a meal delivery service in our community?

- My dad seems depressed since he lost his driver's license. Is counseling available for older persons in the town where he lives? And, is there a way I can arrange transportation for him to get to where he needs to go?

The Eldercare Locator puts callers in touch with services that are available locally. Most communities have social service organizations that are able to provide services to people in need of long-term care. Adult day care and respite care may be offered at a local church or synagogue. Local organizations may sponsor meals-on-wheels programs to feed those who have difficulty caring for themselves. These organizations provide home-delivered meals to homebound persons.

There are also agencies that can arrange for visits to older people. This program, sometimes called Friendly Visiting, helps reduce the loneliness and isolation they may feel. Another service, Telephone Reassurance, provides regular phone contact to the homebound person, so as to check on their safety and well-being. If calls are not answered, a contact person is notified.

A not-for-profit agency in one county offers many services for seniors. It provides non-emergency medical transportation, mobile visual eyecare and home health services. The organization also provides adult day care, legal advice and assistance with shopping.

STATE AGENCIES

Every state has government offices that deal with issues affecting older people (see Appendix B). For example, the New York State Office for the Aging and many other government offices deal with issues affecting the elderly in their state. In Tallahassee, Florida, the state capitol, you will find the Department of Elder Affairs deals with many of the same issues.

Every state also has programs to help the elderly and those in need of long-term care. A limited number of states support a program called Partnership for Long-Term Care. Participants in this program review long-term care policies and issue a seal of approval for those that meet strict consumer standards. They will answer questions and discuss options, but will not recommend a particular policy or company.

Many states have a long-term care ombudsman program. Trained and certified volunteers and professional staff visit long-term care facilities. They investigate complaints and act as advocates for the residents. Disputes can also be mediated through the program.

In Florida, complaints can be filed with the Long-Term Care Ombudsman Council. The Council deals with complaints against nursing homes, adult assisted living facilities, adult family care homes or any licensed long-term care facility. According to the Health Care Financing Administration (HCFA), the Federal agency that oversees Medicare and Medicaid, there are over 500 local ombudsman programs across the country.

HCFA also advises that there are others who may be of assistance for those who are in need of long-term care. They are:

- Hospital discharge planners or social workers;
- Physicians who serve the elderly;
- Clergy and religious organizations;
- Volunteer groups that work with the elderly and chronically ill; and
- Nursing home professional associations.

INSURANCE AND LEGAL HELP

When someone reaches the stage in life when additional care is needed, a great many insurance issues may arise. The federal government funds insurance counseling programs. In addition, state insurance regulators provide a great deal of information in regard to long-term care insurance, and they can also help with health insurance, Medicare and medigap problems. Appendix A provides the phone numbers and addresses of the regulators in your state who may help with problems involving long-term care insurance.

No matter where you live, contact your local state legislator or Congressperson. These people can help you locate the right governmental office that might be able to lend assistance to the individual in need of long-term care. Your representative can assist in cutting through the bureaucracy to find the appropriate agency to help resolve your problem.

GERIATRIC CARE MANAGERS

If you are far away from the person who needs long-term care, a geriatric care manager might be another useful person to contact. As the title suggests, the geriatric care manager oversees all of the care-related issues faced by the individual. Sometimes these individuals are called eldercare managers or senior care managers, but no matter what term is used to describe them, they can be an enormous help when you live far away from the person in need of long-term care.

The geriatric care manager can arrange for the appropriate health or nursing home care for your loved one. A knowledgeable geriatric care manager will know the best facilities in the area, as well as the cost of each and the entrance requirements. The individual should be skilled in crisis intervention. Often, the geriatric care manager will be called upon to help with money management or to cut through the Medicare and Medicaid bureaucracy. The geriatric care manager can bridge the gap between yourself and the person in need of long-term care.

Choosing a geriatric care manager is difficult. You want someone who is thoroughly familiar with available local resources. Also, you want to be comfortable with the person. You need to be able to trust the individual's judgment.

A good starting point is to contact the National Association of Professional Geriatric Care Managers. Members of this group must have at least two years of geriatric experience. The organization has developed voluntary standards and a code of ethics. They are located in Tucson, Arizona, and the phone number to reach them is 520-881-8008. The website is *http://www.caremanager.org*.

Check the credentials of the person you hire. Many geriatric care managers have a background in social work, psychology, gerontology or nursing. A large number of them have done graduate work in their chosen field. The eldercare or geriatric care manager will charge anywhere from $60 to $150 per hour, depending upon his or her credentials.

These care managers can help you make the best decision for your loved one. Sometimes you, as child or spouse, are simply too personally involved to make the best decision.

OTHER SOURCES FOR ASSISTANCE

As the time approaches when long-term care becomes necessary, the right lawyer will be of great assistance. For instance, you may need an elder law attorney to review the contract at a continuing care or life care community. There may also be Medicaid issues that require the services of an attorney. It is also particularly important to resolve issues involving estate planning, living wills, powers of attorney, living trusts and other matters at this time. If you cannot get a recommendation from someone you trust regarding a good lawyer within this specialty, you can check with your local bar association or contact the National Academy of Elder Law Attorneys for the names of attorneys in your area.

In many areas, you do not need to hire a private attorney for assistance. There are programs that arrange legal assistance for the elderly who meet certain income restrictions. Some areas offer legal advice via phone hotlines for older Americans who are unable to come to a legal office.

There are both private and public organizations that address the problems of older adults. A hospital in Boynton Beach, Florida, runs a program for seniors who are experiencing feelings of emptiness, guilt, anxiety and depression. There is no doubt that depression can prompt the need for long-term care. A private business in West Palm Beach offers senior day care. Along with meals, they provide activities for enrollees. The organization will even pick up participants at their residence in the morning and drive them home in the evening. These kinds of programs can be found in many cities.

In areas where there is a high concentration of older adults, you often can find services that help you find the right assisted or independent living facility. If there is no charge for this service, it is highly probable that they are marketing agents for certain facilities. As a result, you will be steered to the facilities they represent. You should always asks who funds a particular service.

A different organization calls itself a placement service and advertises that it offers a free social service. The advertisement says they evaluate hundreds of homes and facilities. In the small print, you will see the service is a facilities contract provider. They are acting as a marketing agent for nursing homes and assisted living facilities.

Businesses have cropped up to help older Americans with the paperwork associated with health insurance claims as well. You can usually find these businesses in your phone book under Insurance Claim Processing Services. Calling (800) 659-3171 will put you in touch with a business in your area that provides this service. Always make certain of the fee beforehand and make sure you are comfortable that the person has the expertise you need.

There are also Web sites that offer advice to those who experience problems in this area. You can tap into the Medicare and Medicaid Web site through *http://www.seniorlink.com* or through other website addresses listed in Appendix C. Housing options are discussed in the University of Georgia Gerontology Web site at *http://omega. geron.uga.edu*, for one. Be wary of certain Web sites, however, because the information may not be objective and it may be sponsored by an individual who is in the business of selling some service for the elderly.

Some long-term care insurers offer assistance as a perk for buying the policy. After buying a policy, you have access to qualified advisers who can offer advice, information and referrals. These advisers help the family make decisions about long-term care.

For additional contacts and resources, please refer to the appendices at the end of this book.

Key Points: The Short Course on Long-Term Care Insurance

- *If you are only going to remember one phone number when you or someone you love needs long-term care, it should be the Eldercare Locator. The phone number is (800) 677-1116.*

- *Geriatric care or eldercare managers can help you locate the right type of long-term care for a loved one. Although the fees may be steep, they can help you find a care arrangement that meets your family's needs. If you cannot afford to hire somebody, social workers and health care professionals can also be a valuable source of information.*

- *The best time to meet with an attorney to address important legal issues related to aging is before someone needs long-term care.*

- *The Family and Medical Leave Act may protect you if you need time off to arrange care for a loved one. In addition, many companies offer access to Employee Assistance Programs. EAP counselors can offer advice on the options available for the person in need of long-term care. They can also offer moral support, which may be desperately needed.*

Chapter 17

CLOSING THE LOOP

"In my mind, Mother is always 50 —healthy, cheerful and supportive. When I call her long distance or write a letter, that is the person I am conversing with. Mom was the one we ran to with our problems. She was never too busy to listen. No matter how muddled things were, she always came up with a logical solution that was acceptable to everyone.

"Now when I see my mother, slightly stooped, clasping the banister tightly before she attempts the challenge of the next step, I turn my head. It pains me to see that she is really getting old.

"Why does my mother's aging bother me so? Why don't I accept the reality that is clearly before me? Because to do so would be to acknowledge that one day I will lose her. One day, I will dial her number as I've done a thousand times before, and she will no longer be there to answer. I refuse to accept the thought of her not being there for me. It is too painful. I can't bear to think about it."[1]

The letter above was written to Ann Landers, the advice columnist. Unfortunately, these are issues we all *must* deal with, especially those of us who truly love our parents and feel blessed they have been with us for as many years as they have. Before the point in time comes when no one answers that phone, you may need to be there for your mother, father or other loved one. The time may be coming when you need to find the best long-term care for someone who has always been there for you.

A PERSONAL MESSAGE

Throughout this book, suggestions have been offered to prepare for the day when long-term care is necessary for you or a loved one. Whether you are in the same town or live across the country, taking care of someone you love is one of the hardest jobs in the world. This book has tried to discuss options and possible solutions. Long-term care insurance is one of the ways to make the best of what may be the most difficult time of your life.

I have tried to provide an objective assessment of the pros and cons of long-term care insurance. I'm often asked if long-term care insurance is worth buying. As I have stated numerous times before, it depends upon your individual situation. No one is making you buy a long-term care insurance policy, unlike auto or homeowners insurance. True, you are taking a risk by not buying it, but none of us buys insurance to guard against every risk we may possibly encounter.

As a general rule, I believe in long-term care insurance, but with certain caveats. I believe in it, as long as you know what the potential problems are and you make the purchase with your eyes wide open. My position is based as much on my own philosophy as it is on the benefits, so you may disagree with my conclusions.

Obviously, there are good and bad policies, good and bad long-term care insurers, and good and bad agents. If you get stuck with a bad one, there is no point in even having long-term care insurance. I hope that after reading this book, you will be able to tell the difference.

Another caveat is that you should not buy long-term care insurance if the premiums will make you give up some of the things you love to do in life. Recognize that the wonderful price you are paying now may go up at some point, even if the premium is based upon your age at the time of purchase. As mentioned, insurance companies do not yet have enough experience to know how to price these policies. Until they see how often they are utilized and to what extent, these policies may be underpriced. State regulators will have little choice but to approve rate increases, unless they want to see some insurance companies go belly-up.

One reason I like long-term care insurance is because I do not believe people in need of long-term care should depend upon Medicaid. Although there are ways to shift assets to qualify for Medicaid, the program is not supposed to be a substitute for long-term care insurance. In addition, I believe your goal should be to have a wide choice of long-term care options.

I do not believe that it is your duty to pass as much wealth as possible to the next generation. The money is there to ensure *your* quality of life for as long as possible. You should not accept a lower quality of care, just so there will be more money for a relative to squander after you have passed away. You have earned it. Spend it in good health. Or, if you can't spend it in good health, use it so you will get the quality of care you deserve.

My advice is to buy as large a daily benefit as possible, even if you must lengthen the elimination period to do so. Long-term care insurance is protection against a catastrophic loss. It may hurt you financially to pick up long-term care expenses while waiting out the elimination period, but it should not bankrupt you. Similarly, it is better to suffer through a long elimination period than to buy a policy that pays benefits for only a year or two. Try for three years at a minimum.

My position in favor of buying long-term care insurance is not based entirely on the financial benefits you might reap in relation to the premiums paid. A case could be made that you are better off *self*-insuring against the risk of needing long-term care. By putting away money in a tax-sheltered account, you might be better off than by paying an insurance company the same amount in premiums.

In theory, you can make the same argument with any insurance policy. Knock-on-wood, my wife and I have not needed to file a claim under our homeowners policy during the 23 years we have owned homes. That fact does not mean that buying homeowners insurance was a bad decision. Obviously, too, the banks that held our mortgage would not have abided by our decision to self-insure. Although our insurance company made money on us, my wife and I, as well as our banks, received a whole lot of peace of mind from the premiums.

You really cannot put a dollar value on that benefit. While I was working for the Pennsylvania Insurance Department, I helped an elderly woman evaluate appropriate long-term care policies, and she still thanks me every time I hear from her. She has never used the policy and hopes never to use it. Nonetheless, she sleeps better knowing she has it. The premium is small when it is compared to the comfort it gives her.

A LONG-TERM PHILOSOPHY REGARDING LONG-TERM CARE

According to one estimate, more than 60 percent of the nursing home residents in our country never have a visitor. Across the country, organizations are starting programs to train and recruit volunteers to visit the elderly and others who reside in nursing homes. Other groups conduct programs to entertain residents. Maybe we should all consider engaging in these efforts

Perhaps it is time to stop searching for programs on television, and instead get up and search for programs in your community that help people in need of long-term care. If there are services that take meals to shut-ins, consider volunteering your time or making a small donation. Lend a hand to a not-for-profit organization that tries to help victims of Alzheimer's disease. Offer to help someone you know who never gets a break from providing long-term care to a relative.

If nothing else, take a few minutes out of your day to call or visit someone you know who is a shut-in. If you are not overwhelmed with work or providing care for your own family, see if there is anything you can bring them or help with. When you are running to the store, see if that person needs an item or two and drop it off. And if all else fails, listen to the commercial and send a card or note to an elderly neighbor who does not seem to have anyone who cares.

Think, but don't dwell, about the day when there may not be anyone left who cares about you and when you may be depending upon others for care. Savor the precious time you have now, but plan for the stage in life that awaits us all. And, if you are walking through a nursing home to visit a loved one, take a moment to talk to a resident or to hold a stranger's extended hand.

Appendix A

STATE INSURANCE OFFICES

Alabama

Insurance Department
201 Monroe St., #1700
Montgomery, AL 36104
(334) 269-3550
Insurance Counseling Program: (800) 243-5463

Alaska

Division of Insurance
3601 C St. Suite 1324
Anchorage, AK 99503-5948
(907) 269-7900 or (800) 467-8725

Arizona

Insurance Department
2910 N. 44th St., #210
Phoenix, AZ 85018
(602) 912-8444
Insurance Counseling Program: (800) 432-4040

Arkansas

Insurance Department
1200 W. 3rd St.
Little Rock, AR 72201
(501) 371-2600
Insurance Counseling Program: (800) 852-5494

California

Insurance Department
Ronald Reagan Building
300 S. Spring St.
Los Angeles, CA 90013
(213) 897-8921
Insurance Counseling Program: (916) 323-7315

Colorado

Insurance Division
1560 Broadway, Suite 850
Denver, CO 80202
(303) 894-7499
Insurance Counseling Program: (303) 894-7499

Connecticut

Insurance Department
153 Market St.
P.O. Box 816
Hartford, CT 06103
(860) 297-3800 or (800) 203-3447
Insurance Counseling Program: (860) 297-3610

Delaware

Insurance Department
Rodney Building
841 Silver Lake Blvd.
Dover, DE 19904
(302) 739-4251 or (800) 282-8611
Insurance Counseling Program: (800) 223-8074

District of Columbia

Insurance Department
513 G St. NW, Room 638
P.O. Box 37200
Washington, DC 20001-7200
(202) 727-8000
Insurance Counseling Program: (202) 724-5626

Florida

Department of Insurance
200 E. Caines St.
Tallahassee, FL 32399-0300
(850) 922-3100 or (800) 342-2762
Insurance Counseling Program: (850) 922-3130

Georgia

Insurance Department
2 Martin Luther King, Jr., Drive
716 West Tower
Atlanta, GA 30334
(404) 656-2056
Insurance Counseling Program: (404) 657-258

Guam

Insurance and Banking Department
855 W. Marine Dr.
P.O. Box 2796
Agana, Guam 96910
(671) 475-1801

Hawaii

Department of Commerce and Consumer Affairs
Insurance Division
250 S. King St., 5th Floor
Honolulu, HI 96813
or:
P.O. Box 3614
Honolulu, HI 96811
(808) 586-2790
Insurance Counseling Program: (808) 586-0100

Idaho

Insurance Department
Public Service Department
700 W. State St., 3rd Floor
Boise, ID 83720
(208) 334-4350
Insurance Counseling Program: (800) 247-4422

Illinois

Insurance Department
320 W. Washington St., 4th Floor
Springfield, IL 62767
(217) 782-4515
Insurance Counseling Program: (800) 252-8966

Indiana

Insurance Department
311 W. Washington St., Suite 300
Indianapolis, IN 46204-2787
(800) 622-4461 or (317) 232-2395
Insurance Counseling Program: (800) 452-4800

Iowa

Insurance Division
330 Maple St.
Des Moines, IA 50319
(515) 281-5705
Insurance Counseling Program: (515) 281-5705

Kansas

Insurance Department
420 SW 9th St.
Topeka, KS 66612-1678
(785) 296-3071
(800) 432-2484
Insurance Counseling Program: (800) 432-3535

Kentucky

Insurance Department
215 W. Main St.
P.O. Box 517
Frankfort, KY 40601
(502) 564-3630
Insurance Counseling Program: (502) 564-6930 or (800) 372-2973 (in KY only)

Louisiana

Insurance Department
950 North 5th St.
Baton Rouge, LA 70802
or:
P.O. Box 94214
Baton Rouge, LA 70804-9214
(504) 342-5900
Insurance Counseling Program: (504) 888-5880 or (800) 259-5301 (in LA only)

Maine

Bureau of Insurance
Consumer Division
State House, Station 34
Augusta, ME 04333
(207) 624-8475
Insurance Counseling Program: (207) 624-5335 or (800) 750-5353 (in ME only)

Maryland

Insurance Department
Complaints & Investigation Unit
525 St. Paul Place
Baltimore, MD 21202-2272
(410) 468-2000
Insurance Counseling Program: (800) 243-3425

Massachusetts

Insurance Division
Consumer Services Section
470 Atlantic Ave.
Boston, MA 02210
(617) 521-7777
Insurance Counseling Program: (617) 727-7750

Michigan

Insurance Department
611 W. Ottawa, 2nd Floor
Lansing, MI 48933
or:
P.O. Box 30220
Lansing, MI 48909
(517) 373-0220
Insurance Counseling Program: (517) 373-8230

Minnesota

Insurance Department
Department of Commerce
133 E. 7th St.
St. Paul, MN 55101-2362
Insurance Counseling Program: (800) 882-6262

Mississippi

Insurance Department
Consumer Assistance Division
550 High St.
1804 Walter Sillers Building
Jackson, MS 39201
or:
P.O. Box 79
Jackson, MS 39205
(601) 359-3569

Missouri

Department of Insurance
Consumer Services Section
301 W. High St.
Jefferson City, MO 65101
(800) 726-7390 or (573) 751-2640
Insurance Counseling Program: (800) 726-7390

Montana

Insurance Department
126 North Sanders
Mitchell Building, Room 270
Helena, MT 59620
(406) 444-2040
Insurance Counseling Program: (800) 332-2272

Nebraska

Insurance Department
Terminal Building
941 "O" St., Suite 400
Lincoln, NE 68508
(402) 471-2201 or (402) 471-2306
Insurance Counseling Program: (402) 471-4506

Nevada

Department of Insurance
Consumer Services
1665 Hot Springs Rd., Suite #152
Carson City, NV 89706
(702) 687-4270 or (800) 992-0900
Insurance Counseling Program: (702) 687-4270

New Hampshire

Insurance Department
Life and Health Division
56 Old Suncook Rd.
Concord, NH 03301
(603) 271-2261 or (800) 852-3416 (in NH only)
Insurance Counseling Program: (603) 271-4642

New Jersey

Insurance Department
20 West State St.
Roebling Building, CN325
Trenton, NJ 08625
(609) 292-5363
Insurance Counseling Program: (800) 792-8820 (in NJ only)

New Mexico

Insurance Department
1120 Paseo De Peralta
Santa Fe, NM 87501
or:
P.O. Box 1269
Santa Fe, NM 87504-1269
(505) 827-4500
Insurance Counseling Program: (800) 432-2080 (in NM only)

New York

Insurance Department
25 Beaver St.
New York, NY 10004
(212) 480-2312
Insurance Counseling Program: (800) 342-9871 (in NY only)

North Carolina

Insurance Department
Seniors Health Insurance Information Program (SHIIP)
111 Seaboard Ave.
Raleigh, NC 27604
or:
P.O. Box 26387
Raleigh, NC 27611
(919) 733-0111 or (800) 662-7777 (in NC only)
Insurance Counseling Program: (800) 443-9354 (in NC only)

North Dakota

Insurance Department
Capitol Building, 5th Floor
600 E. Boulevard
Bismarck, ND 58505-0320
(701) 328-2440 or (800) 247-0560
Insurance Counseling Program: (800) 247-0560 (in ND only)

Ohio

Insurance Department
Consumer Services Division
2100 Stella Court
Columbus, OH 43215
(614) 644-2673 or (800) 686-1526
Insurance Counseling Program: (800) 686-1578 (in OH only)

Oklahoma

Insurance Department
3814 N. Santa Fe
Oklahoma City, OK 73118
or:
P.O. Box 53408
Oklahoma City, OK
73152-3408
Insurance Counseling Program: (405) 521-6628

Oregon

Department of Insurance & Finance
Insurance Division - Consumer Advocacy
350 Winter St. NE, #440-2
Salem, OR 97310
(503) 947-7984

Pennsylvania

Insurance Department
Consumer Services Bureau
1321 Strawberry Square
Harrisburg, PA 17120
(717) 787-2317
Insurance Counseling Program: (717) 783-8975

Puerto Rico

Insurance Department
Femandez Juncos Station Elderly Affairs
P.O. Box 8330
Santurce, PR 00910
(787) 722-8686
Insurance Counseling Program: (787) 721-5710

Rhode Island

Insurance Division
233 Richmond St., Suite 233
Providence, RI 02903-4233
(401) 222-2223
Insurance Counseling Program: (800) 322-2880 (in PR only)

South Carolina

Insurance Department
Consumer Assistance
1612 Marion St.
Columbia, SC 29202
or:
P.O. Box 100105
Columbia, SC 29202-3105
(803) 737-6160
Insurance Counseling Program: (800) 868-9095 (in SC only)

South Dakota

Insurance Department
118 West Capitol
Pierre, SD 57501-5070
(605) 773-3563
Insurance Counseling Program: (605) 773-3656

Tennessee

Department of Commerce & Insurance
Insurance Assistance
500 James Roberston Pkwy., 4th Floor
Nashville, TN 37243-0574
(615) 741-4955 or (800) 525-2816

Texas

Department of Insurance
Complaints Resolution, MC 111-1A
333 Guadalupe St.
P.O. Box 149104
Austin, TX 78714-9104
(512) 463-6515 or (800) 252-3439
Insurance Counseling Program: (800) 252-9240

Utah

Insurance Department
Consumer Services
3110 State Office Building
Salt Lake City, UT 84114-1201
(801) 538-3805 or (800) 439-3805
Insurance Counseling Program: (801) 538-3910

Vermont

Department of Banking & Insurance
Consumer Complaint Division
89 Main St., Drawer 20
Montpelier, VT 05602
(802) 828-3301
Insurance Counseling Program: (800) 642-5119 (in VT only)

Virginia

Bureau of Insurance, Consumer Services Division
1300 East Main St.
P.O. Box 1157
Richmond, VA 23219
(804)371-9694
Insurance Counseling Program: (800) 552-4464 (in VA only)

Virgin Islands

Insurance Department
Kongens Gade, No. 18
St. Thomas, VI 00802
(340) 774-2991
Insurance Counseling Program: (340) 774-2991

Washington

Insurance Department
Insurance Building
14th & Water St.
Olympia, WA 98504
or:
P.O. Box 40255
Olympia, WA 98504-0255
(360) 753-7300 or (800) 562-6900 (in WA only)

West Virginia

Insurance Department
1124 Smith St.
Charleston, WV 25301
(304) 558-3386 or (800) 642-9004 (in WV only)
For hearing impaired: (800) 435-7381 (in WV only)
Insurance Counseling Program: (304) 558-3317

Wisconsin

Insurance Department
Complaints Department
121 E. Wilson St.
Madison, WI 53702
or:
P.O. Box 7873
Madison, WI 53707-7873
(608) 266-0103 or (800) 236-8517
Insurance Counseling Program: (800) 242-1060 (in WI only)

Wyoming

Insurance Department
Herschler Building
122 W. 25th St.
Cheyenne, WY 82002
(307) 777-7401 or (800) 438-5768
Insurance Counseling Program: (800) 438-5768 (in WY only)

Appendix B

AGENCIES ON AGING

NATIONAL

National Association of State Units on Aging
1225 I St., NW, Suite 725
Washington, DC 20005
(202) 898-2578

National Association of Area Agencies on Aging
927 15th St. NW, 6th Floor
Washington, DC 20005
(202) 296-8130

STATE

Alabama

Commission on Aging
770 Washington Ave., Suite 470
Montgomery, AL 36130-1851
(800) 243-5463 or (334) 242-5743

Alaska

Older Alaskans Commission
P.O. Box 110209
Juneau, AK 99811-0209
(907) 465-3250

American Samoa

Territorial Administration on Aging
Government of American Somoa
Pago Pago, AS 96799
633-1251 (from the states: 011-684-633-1251)

Arizona

Department of Economic Security
Aging & Adult Administration
1789 W. Jefferson St., #950A
Phoenix, AZ 85007
(602) 542-4446

Arkansas

Division of Aging and Adult Services
1417 Donaghey Plaza South
P.O. Box 1437/Slot 1412
Little Rock, AR 72203-1437
(501) 682-2441 or (800) 852-5494

California

Department of Aging
1600 K Street
Sacramento, CA 95814
(916) 322-3887 or (800) 510-2020 (in CA only)

Colorado

Aging and Adult Services
Department of Social Services
110 16th St., #200
Denver, CO 80202
(303) 620-4147 or (800) 576-6111

Connecticut

Department on Aging
10 Prospect St.
Hartford, CT 06103
(860) 543-8690

Delaware

Division of Aging
Department of Health & Social Services
1901 N. DuPont Highway
2nd Floor Annex, Admin. Bldg.
New Castle, DE 19720
(302) 577-4781 or (800) 223-9074

District of Columbia

Office on Aging
441 4th St. NW
Suite 950 N.
Washington, DC 20001
(202) 724-5626

Florida

Department of Elder Affairs
4040 Esplanade Way
Suite 152
Tallahassee, FL 32399-7000
(850) 414-2000

Georgia

Office of Aging
Department of Human Resources
132 Mitchell St., 2nd Floor
Atlanta GA 30303
(404) 730-0184

Guam

Division of Senior Citizens
Department of Public Health and Social Services
P.O. Box 2816
Agana, Guam 96910
(671) 475-0263

Hawaii

Department of Commerce
Executive Office on Aging and Consumer Affairs
250 S. Hotel St., #109
Honolulu, HI 96813-2831
(808) 586-0100

Idaho

Office on Aging
3380 Americana Terr., Suite 120
Boise, ID 83706
(208) 334-3833

Illinois

Department on Aging
421 E. Capitol Avenue
Springfield, IL 62701
(217) 785-3356
(800) 252-8966 (in IL only)

Indiana

Division of Aging and Home Services
402 W. Washington St., Room #W-454
P.O. Box 7083
Indianapolis, IN 46207-7083
(317) 232-7020 or (800) 545-7763

Iowa

Department of Elder Affairs
210th St., 3rd Floor
Des Moines, IA 50309-3609
(515) 281-5187
(800) 532-3213 (in IA only)

Kansas

Department on Aging
New England Building
5503 S. Kansas
Topeka, KS 66603-3404
(785) 296-4986
(800) 432-3535 (in KS only)

Kentucky

Division of Aging Services
Cabinet for Human Resources
275 E. Main St. - 5WA
Frankfort, KY 40621
(502) 564-6930

Louisiana

Governor's Office of Elderly Affairs
412 N. 4th St., 3rd Floor
Baton Rouge, LA 70802
or:
P.O. Box 80374
Baton Rouge, LA 70898-0374
(225) 342-7100

Maine

Bureau of Elder and Adult Services
35 Anthony Ave.
11 State House Station
Augusta, ME 04333
(207) 624-5335

Maryland

Office on Aging
301 W. Preston St., Room 1007
Baltimore, MD 21201
(410) 767-1100
(800) 243-3425 (in MD only)

Massachusetts

Executive Office of Elder Affairs
1 Ashburton Pl., 5th Floor
Boston, MA 02108
(800) 882-2003 or (617) 727-7750

Michigan

Office of Services to the Aging
Ottawa Building, 3rd Floor
611 West Ottawa St.
Lansing, MI 48933
or:
P.O.Box 30676
Lansing, MI 48909-8176
(517) 373-8230

Minnesota

Board on Aging
Human Services Building, 4th Floor
444 Lafayett Rd.
St. Paul, MN 55155-3843
(612) 296-2770 or (800) 882-6262

Mississippi

Division of Aging and Adult Services
750 N. State St.
Jackson, MS 39202
(800) 948-3090 or (601) 359-4929

Missouri

Division of Aging
Dept. of Social Services
P.O. Box 1337
615 Howerton Court
Jefferson City, MO 65109
(573) 751-3082
(800) 392-0210 (in MO only)

Montana

Governor's Office on Aging
State Capitol Building, Room 219
Helena, MT 59620-0801
(800) 332-2272 or (406) 444-3111

Nebraska

Department on Aging
State Office Building
301 Centenniel Mall South
Lincoln, NE 68509-5044
(402) 471-2306

Nevada

Department of Human Resources
Division for Aging Services
340 N. 11th St., Suite 203
Las Vegas, NV 89101
(702) 486-3545

New Hampshire

Dept. of Health & Human Services
Division of Elderly & Adult Services
State Office Park S.
115 Pleasant St., Annex Bldg. #1
Concord, NH 03301
(603) 271-4680
(800) 351-1888 (in NH only)

New Jersey

Department of Community Affairs
Division on Aging
Quaker Bridge Plaza
P.O. Box 807
Trenton, NJ 08625-0807
(800) 792-8820 or (609) 588-3139

New Mexico

State Agency on Aging
La Villa Rivera Bldg.
228 E. Palace Ave.
Santa Fe., NM 87501
(800) 432-2080 or (505) 827-7640

New York

State Office for the Aging
Two Empire State Plaza
Albany, NY 12223-1251
(800) 342-9871 or (518) 474-5731

North Carolina

Division of Aging
693 Palmer Dr., Caller Box 29531
Raleigh, NC 27626-0531
(919) 733-3983
(800) 662-7030 (in NC only)

North Dakota

Department of Human Services
Aging Services Division
600 S. 2nd St., Suite 1
Bismarck, ND 58504
(701) 328-8910
(800) 472-2622 (in ND only)

Ohio

Department of Aging
50 W. Broad St., 8th Floor
Columbus, OH 43215-5928
(614) 466-1221

Oklahoma

Department of Human Services
Aging Services Division
312 NE 28th St.
Oklahoma City, OK 73105
(405) 521-2327

Oregon

Department of Human Resources
Senior and Disabled Services Division
500 Summer St., NE, 2nd Floor
Salem, OR 97310-1015
(800) 282-8096 or (503) 945-5811

Pennsylvania

Department of Aging
555 Walnut St., 5th Floor
Harrisburg, PA 17101-1919
(717) 783-1550

Puerto Rico

Governor's Office for Elderly Affairs
Gericulture Commission
La Fortaleza
P.O. Box 9020082
San Juan, PR 00902
(787) 721-7000

Rhode Island

Department of Elderly Affairs
160 Pine St.
Providence, RI 02903
(401) 222-2858
(800) 322-2880 (in RI only)

South Carolina

Commission on Aging
1801 Main St., 10th Floor
Columbia, SC 29202-8206
(803) 253-6177

South Dakota

Office of Adult Services and Aging
700 Governor's Drive
Pierre, SD 57501-2291
(605) 773-3656

Tennessee

Commission on Aging
500 Deaderick St.
Andrew Jackson Building, 9th Floor
Nashville, TN 37243-0860
(615) 741-2056

Texas

Department on Aging
4900 N. Lamar
Austin, TX 78751
(512) 424-6840
(800) 252-9240 (in TX only)

Utah

Division of Aging & Adult Services
120 North 200 W., Room 401
P.O. Box 45500
Salt Lake City, UT 84103
(801) 538-3910

Vermont

Department of Aging and Disabilities
Waterbury Complex
103 S. Main St.
Waterbury, VT 05671-2301
(802) 241-2400

Virginia

Department for the Aging
1600 Forest Ave., #102
Richmond, VA 23229
(804) 662-9333
(800) 552-4464 (in VA only)
Long-Term Care Ombudsman Program: (800) 552-3402 (in VA only)

Virgin Islands

Senior Citizens Affairs Division
19 Estate Diamond
Fredericksted
St. Croix, VI 00840
(340) 774-0930

Washington

Aging & Adult Services Administration
600 Woodland Square Loop SE
Building A
Lacey, WA 98503
or:
P.O. Box 40505
Department of Social Services
Olympia, WA 98504-5050
(360) 493-2500
(800) 422-3263 (in WA only)

West Virginia

Commission on Aging
State Capitol Complex
Holly Grove - Building 10
1900 Kanawha Blvd. East
Charleston, WV 25305-0160
(304) 558-3317

Wisconsin

Bureau of Aging & Long-Term Care Resources
Department of Health & Social Services
P.O. Box 7851
One W. Wilson St.
Madison, WI 53707-7851
(608) 266-2536

Wyoming

Commission on Aging
Hathaway Building, Room 139
2300 Capitol Ave.
Cheyenne, WY 82002
(800) 442-2766 or (307) 777-7986

Appendix C

ADDITIONAL RESOURCES

NATIONAL ORGANIZATIONS

Alzheimer's Disease Education and Referral Center

P.O. Box 8250
Silver Spring, MD 20907-8250
(800) 438-4380
http://www.alzheimers.org

Alzheimer's Association National Office

919 N. Michigan Ave.
Suite 1000
Chicago, IL 60611-1676
(800) 272-3900
(312) 335-8700
http://www.alz.org

American Association of Homes and Services for the Aging

901 E. Street N.W.
Suite 500
Washington, DC 20004-2011
(202) 783-2242
http://www.aahsa.org

American Association of Retired People (AARP)

601 E Street NW
Washington, DC 20049
(800) 424-3410
http://www.aarp.org

American Health Care Association

1201 L St., N.W.
Washington, DC 20005
(202) 842-4444

Assisted Living Federation of America

10300 Eaton Place
Suite 400
Fairfax, VA 22030
(703) 691-8100
http://www.alfa.org

Health Insurance Association of America

555 13th St. N.W.
Suite 600 E
Washington, DC 20004
(202) 824-1600
http://www.hiaa.org

National Association of Area Agencies on Aging

927 5th St. NW
6th Floor
Washington, DC 20005
(202) 297-8130
Eldercare Locator: (800) 677-1116

National Association of Insurance Commissioners (NAIC)

120 W. 12th St.

Suite 1100

Kansas City, MO 64105-1925

(816) 942-3600

http://www.naic.org

Comprised of chief insurance regulators in all 50 states, the District of Columbia, and U.S. territories. The NAIC helps state regulators to protect the interest of insurance consumers, provides a forum for developing public policy which states are invited to adopt.

National Association of Professional Geriatric Care Managers

1604 N. Country Road

Tucson, AZ 85716-3102

(520) 881-8008

http://www.caremanager.org

National Center for Home Equity Conversion

360 N. Robert, #403

St. Paul, MN 55101

(651) 222-6775

(651) 222-6797 (Fax)

http://www.reverse.org

National Citizens' Coalition for Nursing Home Reform

1424 16th St. N.W.

Suite 202

Washington, DC 20036-2211

(202) 332-2275

National Institute on Aging

Information Center

P.O. Box 8057

Gaithersburg, MD 20898-8057

(800) 222-2225

(800) 222-4225 (TTY)

http://www.nih.gov/nia/

Nursing Home Information Service

c/o National Council of Senior Citizens

8403 Colesville Rd.

Suite 1200

Silver Spring, MD 20910

(301) 578-8938

http://www.ncscinc.org

Information on community services and free guide on how to select a nursing home.

U.S. Department of Housing and Urban Development (HUD)

451 7th Street SW

Washington, DC 20410

http://www.hud.gov/

United Seniors Health Cooperative

409 3rd St. SW

Suite 200

Washington, DC 20024

(202) 479-6973

LEGAL SERVICES FOR THE ELDERLY

American Association of Retired Persons

Legal Services Network
P.O. Box 100084
Pittsburgh, PA 15290
or, National Office:
AARP
601 E. Street, N.W.
Washington, DC 20049
(800) 424-3410
http://www.aarp/lsn

American Bar Association
Commission on Legal Problems of the Elderly

740 15th Street, N.W.
Washington, DC 20005-1022
(202) 662-8690

American Society on Aging

83 Market St.
Suite 511
San Francisco, CA 94103
(415) 974-9600

Gerontological Society of America

1030 15th St. NW
Suite 250
Washington, DC 20005
(202) 842-1275

Gray Panthers

733 15th St. NW
Suite 437
Washington, DC 20005
(202) 737-6637

National Academy of Elder Law Attorneys

1604 N. Country Club Rd.
Tucson, AZ 85716-3102
(520) 881-4005
http://www.naela.org

National Caucus and Center on Black Aged

1424 K Street, NW
Suite 500
Washington, DC 20005
(202) 637-8400

National Citizen's Coalition for Nursing Home Reform

1424 16th St. NW
Suite 202
Washington, DC 20036-2211
(202) 332-2275

National Senior Citizen Law Center

1101 14th St., NW
Suite 400
Washington, DC 20005
(202) 289-6976

PUBLICATIONS ON LONG-TERM CARE INSURANCE

"A Shoppers Guide to Long-Term Care Insurance"

Includes worksheets to guide you through the decision-making process. You can get it for free from your state insurance regulator or by writing the NAIC Publications Department, Box 263, Kansas City, MO 64193.

"Guide to Health Insurance for People with Medicare."

From the Health Care Financing Administration. Call (800) 638-6833, or look on the web at *http://www.hcfa.gov/.*

"Guide to Long-term Care Insurance"

Order from: Health Insurance Association of America, Publications Office (see address above under Agencies, phone (202) 824-1600). Available on-line at *http://www.hiaa.org/consumerinfo/guideltc.html.*

"Long-Term Care Insurance: To Buy or Not to Buy"

Available for $2 from the non-profit consumer group United Seniors Health Cooperative (see address listed above under National Organizations, phone (202) 479-6973).

"Long-Term Care Planning: A Dollar and Sense Guide"

Available for $15 from the United Seniors Health Cooperative (see address listed above under Agencies, phone (202) 479-6973).

WEB SITES OF INTEREST

Government Services and Related:

Administration on Aging
http://www.aoa.dhhs.gov/

Area Agencies on Aging (from the Administration on Aging)
http://www.aoa.dhhs.gov/aoa/webres/area-agn.htm

Department of Health and Human Services

http://www.os.dhhs.gov/

Health Care Financing Administration

http://www.hcfa.gov/

Insure.com (Insurance News Network)

http://www.insure.com

National Institute on Aging of the National Institutes of Health

http://www.nih.gov/nia

Medicare Online Consumer Information

http://www.medicare.gov/

Medicaid Consumer Information

http://www.hcfa.gov/medicaid/mcaicnsm.htm

Medicaid Long Term Care Services

http://www.hcfa.gov/medicaid/ltchomep.htm

Pension and Welfare Benefits Administration

http://www.dol.gov/dol/pwba/

Pension Benefit Guaranty Corp

http://www.pbgc.gov/

Social Security Online

http://www.ssa.gov/

Veterans Affairs Department

http://www.va.gov

Long-Term Care Insurance:

National Association of Insurance Commissioners

http://www.naic.org/

Directory of State Long Term Care Ombudsman Programs

http://www.aoa.dhhs.gov/aoa/pages/ltcomb.html

The Long Term Care Insurance Info Page

http://www.ltc-info.com

Contains a free guide to long-term care insurance with article reprints, worksheets, glossary, a list of resources, Frequently Asked Questions, Links to government, insurance, seniors, healthcare and other pages.and more.

Mr. Long Term Care

http://www.mr-longtermcare.com

Housing Issues:

Eldercare Locator Database

http://www.ageinfo.org/elderloc/

C/o the National Aging Information Center.

Housing Options for the Aging

University of Georgia Gerontology Web site
http://omega.geron.uga.edu

Senior Living Alternatives Guide

http://www.senioralternatives.com

New York State Office for the Aging

http://www.aging.state.ny.us/nysofa/homa.htm

California Registry's Online Senior Housing and Senior Care Database

http://www.calregistry.com/

Of General Interest to Senior Citizens:

American Association of Retired People Webplace

http://www.aarp.org

Elderweb

http://www.elderweb.com

Government Information Xchange/Senior Citizen Information

http://www.info.gov/Info/html/senior_citizens.htm

SeniorsSearch Announcement Pages

http://www.seniorssearch.com

Caregiver Information and Support:

Extended Care Information Network

http://www.extendedcare.com/Eldercare/public/main.html

Today's Caregiver Online

http://www.caregiver.com/

Appendix D

GLOSSARY

accelerated death benefit: A life insurance policy provision that lets you take an advance on the policy's death benefit, if certain conditions are met, to pay for long-term care.

activities of daily living: The activities of daily living, or ADLs, are usually the basis for the benefits eligibility trigger in the long-term care policy. The policy will stipulate that it won't pay, unless you are unable to perform a specified number of the ADLs. The ADLs are now the common standard for measuring whether someone is eligible to collect benefits under a long-term care policy. Typical ADLs are eating, continence, bathing, toileting, dressing and transferring from bed to chair or wheelchair.

acute care: Unlike chronic care, acute care is short-term medical treatment for a serious injury or illness. It is usually administered in a hospital or skilled nursing facility.

adult day care centers: Centers that are often run by non-profit agencies and the cost is sometimes based upon ability to pay. Adult day care centers run on the same principle as day care for children. They are open during customary business hours, so caregivers can go to work and administer long-term care during evenings and weekends.

aging in place: A term used to describe the usual preference for continuing to live in one's own home environment.

Alzheimer's disease: A progressive, degenerative illness that affects the brain. The person's cognitive and functional abilities decline gradually over time. Some of the symptoms are memory loss, disorientation, impaired judgment, personality changes, mood swings and behavioral abnormalities. Alzheimer's disease is an organic mental disorder.

Alzheimer's units: Specialized facilities that care for Alzheimer's patients.

Area Agencies on Aging: A local agency, funded through the federal Older Americans Act, that coordinates social service and health programs for persons age 60 and older.

assisted living facilities: Residences that provide personal care and assistance with the activities of daily living.

bed reservation benefit: A benefit often found in a long-term care policy that makes payment so an insured's residence in a nursing home isn't lost while the resident is temporarily hospitalized.

board and care homes: Small, private residential facilities where residents receive all meals, as well as personal care. These homes are not for individuals who need the high level of care available in a nursing home. The care provided is non-medical and custodial in nature. In some areas, they are also referred to as residential care homes.

caregiver: The individual who provides care and companionship to someone on an ongoing basis.

chronic care: Unlike acute care, chronic care is ongoing long-term care.

cognitive impairment: A loss or deterioration in intellectual capacity that is comparable to and includes Alzheimer's disease and similar forms of irreversible dementia. There is impairment in short or long-term memory, orientation as to people, places or time, and deductive or abstract reasoning. Cognitive impairment is a common trigger in long-term care policies. Mental tests are administered.

congregate housing: Housing operated by many different groups. It offers independent living but with some central facilities like a common dining room where meals are served. It is often used interchangeably with the term "senior housing."

continuing care communities: Continuing care and life care communities offer many housing options, from independent living facilities to skilled nursing care. Some have on-site medical personnel, whereas others offer transportation to physicians and other services. Many require an up-front payment, as well as monthly fees. Recently, some communities began offering their services on a rental basis and health care coverage is paid for when needed. Although the terms are often used interchangeably, continuing care communities cannot really be called life care communities unless they guarantee health care coverage for life without exception and residents can always reside there, even if their financial resources are exhausted.

continuum of care: The entire spectrum of care from minimal assistance to substantial assistance.

custodial care: The purpose of custodial care is to meet the personal needs of the patient. The caregiver helps the person perform the activities of daily living such as eating, bathing, dressing or taking medicine. The care might be provided in a nursing home, adult day care center, or at home. Custodial care is provided by people who don't possess medical training.

daily benefit: This is the amount in dollars that will be paid to cover the expense of long-term care, if the insured meets the requirements of the policy.

dementia: The loss or deterioration in intellectual capacity, usually caused by organic brain disease.

durable power of attorney: A legal document that authorizes someone to act as the agent or attorney-in-fact for another person, who is called the principal. The authority continues, even if the principal becomes incapacitated or incompetent. An ordinary power of attorney becomes ineffectual when the principal becomes incompetent or incapacitated. The durable power of attorney must specifically state that it will remain valid, despite the principal's incapacity or incompetence.

durable power of attorney for health care: This power of attorney gives the person you designate the power to make health care decisions for you. The durable power of attorney for health care is only effective if you cannot make those decisions yourself. In some states, it makes more sense to have a living will.

Eldercare Locator: A service that is provided by the Older Americans Act to help consumers locate services for the person in need of long-term care. The telephone number is (800) 677-1116.

elimination period: The waiting period for benefits to begin under a long-term care policy. The longer the elimination period, the cheaper the policy will be.

Employee Assistance Program (EAP): Employee benefit provided by many companies which makes counselors available to advise individuals on long-term care issues, as well as other psychological, financial and medical problems.

exclusion: Language in a long-term care policy that eliminates coverage for a particular occurrence.

Family and Medical Leave Act of 1993 (FLMA): Federal law that permits workers in certain instances to take a leave of absence to care for a relative.

foster care: Care that resembles that assistance provided to a minor in a foster home. The person in need of long-term care lives with someone who can help with the activities of daily living.

free look period: A provision in the long-term care policy, required in many states by insurance regulators, which lets the policyholder review it for a specified period of time. During that free look period, the policy may be returned to the insurer for a refund of the entire premium.

front-end underwriting: The long-term care insurer does a full investigation of the applicant's medical background and application before issuing a policy.

geriatric care manager: This individual deals with issues concerning the elderly. He or she oversees all of the care-related issues of the person who needs long-term care. The geriatric care manager is sometimes called an eldercare manager or a senior care manager.

guaranteed renewable: The insured is permitted to continue the coverage, as long as premiums are paid in a timely manner. Guaranteed renewability also means the premium remains the same, unless there is a premium increase for everyone in that particular rate classification.

guaranty fund: A fund that exists in most states that protects a person dealing with a financially-troubled insurance company. Guaranty funds do not provide absolute protection when an insurance company becomes insolvent.

Health Insurance Portability and Accountability Act of 1996: This federal law established requirements for a long-term policy to be qualified. Only qualified policies entitle the purchaser to tax breaks. Qualified policies must meet certain standards set forth in the Act.

home health care: Home health care is defined as medical and non-medical services provided to ill, disabled or infirm persons in their residences. The home health care category covers skilled nursing care, as well as other services such as therapy or assistance with the activities of daily living.

hospice care: Hospice care provides support for the dying and their families. Some hospice programs let patients stay in their home or create a home-like atmosphere in a special institution. Usually, hospice patients have a life expectancy of six months or less. The hospice worker helps the family cope with the emotional upheaval caused by their situation.

incontestability clause: A provision in a long-term care policy, which says that after a specified period of time, the insurance company may not challenge your entitlement to coverage.

independent living: Housing arrangement for someone who is able to perform the activities of daily living without the assistance of others.

inflation rider: An option purchased with a long-term care policy that increases the benefit each year to keep pace with inflation. There are two types of inflation riders, simple and compound. The compounded inflation rider provides more coverage each year than the simple inflation rider.

informal caregiver benefit: The policy pays for care provided by a friend or relative. In contrast, some policies won't pay caregivers who are related to the insured.

instrumental activities of daily living: The instrumental ADLs include cooking, grocery shopping, laundry, bill paying, telephoning and housekeeping.

intermediate care: Intermediate care requires less than twenty-four hour nursing supervision. It is performed several times a week, or even on a daily basis, for those who have stable conditions. This type of care must also be performed by, or under the supervision of, skilled medical personnel. Intermediate care refers to intermittent medical care, such as giving injections to the patient. The care is provided pursuant to a doctor's orders.

levels of care: Skilled nursing care, intermediate care and custodial care.

level premium: The premium charged at the inception of the policy remains the same throughout the duration of it. Using the term, "level premium," in reference to a long-term care policy may be a misnomer, since the premium may be adjusted if all members of the same group within that state are granted a rate increase.

life care communities: Communities that offer many housing options, from independent living facilities to skilled nursing care. Many require an up-front payment, as well as monthly fees. Some have on-site medical personnel, whereas others offer transportation to physicians and other services. Although the term is sometimes used interchangeably with continuing care communities, a true life care community guarantees residents that they can keep their homes, even if their funds are exhausted.

living will: A document that states in general terms the kind of medical care you want and do not want. Because it takes effect while you are living, it is called a living will. In some states, it may make more sense to have a durable power of attorney for health care.

look-back period: A period of time, usually 36 months or longer, that will be examined when an individual applies for Medicaid. All gifts and transfers during that time frame will be scrutinized to see if they were made to help the individual meet Medicaid's financial guidelines.

long-term care: Ongoing care that includes assistance with the activities of daily living. It might include medical and non-medical services.

Medicaid: A federal program, administered by the states, that pays for care of individuals who meet certain guidelines, usually low income. In certain instances, Medicaid will pay for long-term care in a nursing home or may cover some home health care.

Medical Savings Accounts (MSA): These are tax-sheltered accounts for employees of a small business or the self-employed. There may be a way to pay long-term care insurance premiums out of your MSA and reduce your tax burden at the same time. Your contributions to the MSA may be deductible.

Medicare: Medicare is a federal program which provides hospital and medical insurance for individuals who are over age 65, as well as people of any age with certain disabilities or permanent kidney failure. Medicare won't pay for home health care that is custodial, unless it is related to treatment of an illness or injury. For Medicare to pay, the custodial care must be accompanied by skilled nursing care or therapy.

Medicare supplements: Private policies that are purchased to supplement Medicare. They are also called medigap policies. Medicare supplemental policies only provide limited coverage for long-term care.

medigap policies: Nickname for Medicare supplemental policies. They only provide limited coverage for long-term care.

nonforfeiture benefits: A benefit that returns some of your premiums or keeps a reduced portion of the coverage in force, if you cancel your policy or allow it to lapse.

nursing home: A facility that provides one or more levels of care to persons who need assistance. A nursing home may provide skilled, intermediate and/or custodial care.

Older Americans Act of 1965: A federal law that set up a network of state area agencies on aging. These agencies plan, coordinate and fund local programs for people age 60 and older. Congress has reauthorized the Act on fourteen occasions and made changes to improve programs for Older Americans.

ombudsman program: There are over 500 local ombudsman programs across the country. Individuals visit nursing homes on a regular basis and investigate complaints. The ombudsperson in your area can provide general information about nursing homes.

organic disorder: A change in the structure of an organ caused by disease in contrast to a functional or psychosomatic disorder. Parkinson's and Alzheimer's disease are organic mental disorders, since there is an alteration in the brain's structure.

outline of coverage: A document provided in conjunction with the sale of a long-term care policy that gives an overview of the coverage purchased.

paid-up policy: A type of forfeiture benefit that keeps a reduced amount of coverage in force if you fail to pay the premium.

Parkinson's Disease: A highly complex brain disease that affects physical movement. It has no known cause or cure. The nature and severity of its symptoms can be kept in check with surgery and drugs. The symptoms are normally tremors, muscle rigidity, and a shuffling walk.

post-claims underwriting: An unethical practice by a long-term care insurer where it doesn't investigate the accuracy of the application for coverage until after a claim has been filed. If the company discovers a misrepresentation, it may be able to deny coverage or reject the claim.

power of attorney: Unlike the durable power of attorney, this legal document is no longer valid after the principal becomes incompetent or incapacitated.

pre-existing condition: A medical problem for which the insured was treated, or was aware of, before applying for an insurance policy. All pre-existing conditions should be listed on the application to avoid a coverage problem.

qualified policies: This means the policy is tax-qualified. Under the Health Insurance Portability and Accountability Act of 1996, a long-term care policy must be "qualified" in order for the buyer to take a tax deduction.

residential care homes: Small, private residential facilities where residents receive all meals, as well as personal care. These homes are not for individuals who need the high level of care available in a nursing home. The care provided is non-medical and custodial in nature. In some areas, they are also referred to as board and care homes.

respite care: Respite care is designed to give the primary caregiver a well-deserved rest. When the primary caregiver needs a break from the day-to-day strain of providing long-term care, these services can be utilized.

restoration of benefits: A provision offered by some long-term care policies which restores the policy's full benefit, if no money is paid out for a specified period of time.

retirement community: A community with housing for older individuals. Some retirement communities offer services for the elderly, but are mainly for active and independent seniors. A typical age restriction is age 55 or older.

return of premium benefit: One form of a nonforfeiture benefit that returns some or all of the premiums paid, if not used while the policy is in force. It is usually an option that you must pay extra for when buying a long-term care policy.

rider: An endorsement to an insurance policy that adds or eliminates coverage.

risk management: Looking for potential hazards that may be encountered and taking the appropriate steps to guard against their occurrence.

"sandwich generation": This refers to those individuals who have the dual responsibility of caring for aging parents, while they are raising children. If a parent's health is deteriorating and you have young children, you are providing a great deal of care to each generation.

senior housing: Senior housing is operated by many different groups. It offers independent living but with some central facilities like a common dining room where meals are served. It is often used interchangeably with the term, congregate housing. Some senior apartment complexes are subsidized by the Department of Housing and Urban Development (HUD).

settings of care: The place where care is provided. For example, home health care is provided in the individual's residence.

shared benefit: A feature in a policy that provides long-term care coverage for two insureds and permits them to share the selected benefit if both meet the eligibility requirements.

skilled nursing care: Skilled nursing care is the highest level of care. Skilled nursing care can only be performed by, or under the supervision of, skilled medical personnel. The care must be provided pursuant to a doctor's orders. There must be a treatment plan that the nurses or therapists follow. The skilled nursing care is sometimes performed in the person's home. It is available twenty-four hours a day.

spending down assets: To qualify for Medicaid, applicants must deplete their income and assets to meet the eligibility requirements in their state.

spousal discount: A reduction in premium offered by some insurers when both spouses purchase a long-term care policy.

spousal impoverishment: A rule that protects the spouse of someone eligible for Medicaid who needs care in a nursing home. The spouse who is still in the family home is allowed to keep a specified amount of income and assets. The formula is likely to be different, depending upon the state in which you live.

tax-qualified policy: The Health Insurance Portability and Accountability Act of 1996 established requirements for a long-term policy to be tax-qualified. Only qualified policies entitle the purchaser to tax breaks. Qualified policies must meet certain standards set forth in the Act.

trigger: The standard for measuring whether the insured is entitled to receive benefits.

twisting: The unethical practice where an agent makes a misleading representation or incomplete or fraudulent comparison of policies or insurers for the purpose of inducing a person to buy a different policy.

underwriting: The process that a long-term care insurer uses to decide whether to provide insurance coverage to the applicant.

viatical settlement: Agreement in which terminally ill individuals sell their life insurance policies before they die and get a percentage of the death benefit in cash.

waiver of premium: A feature in an insurance policy which relieves the insured of paying premiums if certain conditions are met. The policy and all of the benefits remain in force, even though premiums are not being paid. Once those conditions are no longer met, the premiums are owed again.

will: A legal document that directs how property is to be distributed at death.

CHAPTER REFERENCES

Chapter 1: Planning for Tomorrow

1. Van Buren, Abigail: "Dear Abby," [Column]. *Pittsburgh-Post Gazette*, May 31, 1998, p. H45.
2. Van Buren, Abigail: "Wife should quit job" [Dear Abby column]. *Sun-Sentinel*, March 11, 1998, p. 2E.

Chapter 2: Housing Options for the Aging

1. Katzberg, William: "The Florida condo growing older, older." *Palm Beach Jewish Journal South*, April 14-20, 1998, p. 17A.
2. Fletcher, June: "Retirees say no to parents' communities." *The Wall Street Journal*, November 14, 1997, p. B14.
3. Lade, Diane C: "College towns: new hot spots for retirement." *Sun-Sentinel*, March 15, 1999, pp. 1A, 6A.
4. Jeter, Jon: "Elderly still seek wisdom at unique college for aged." *Pittsburgh Post-Gazette*, April 19, 1998, p. A17.
5. Reeves, Pamela: "As population ages, housing options expand to accommodate seniors." *Pittsburgh Post-Gazette*, August 9, 1998, p. H5.
6. "Assisted living gains popularity among senior citizens." Online. Available: *http://cnn.com/HEALTH/9808/13/assisted.living.* August 19, 1998.

Chapter 3: What Is Long-Term Care?

1. Brothers, Joyce: "Are you caught in the middle?" *Parade Magazine*, June 28, 1998, pp. 4-6.

2. Landers, Ann: "Group supports right to choose" [Column]. *The Palm Beach Post*, May 17, 1998, p. 25D.

3. Ansberry, Clare: "Who's afraid of aging? Usually not the elderly --they know better." *The Wall Street Journal*, December 31, 1997, A1-2.

4. Lade, Diane C.: "Opinions mixed on nursing-home suit." *Sun-Sentinel*, February 15, 1998, pp. 1B, 6B.

5. "Jury awards $10.7 million in nursing home death." *The Wall Street Journal*, September 15, 1997, p. B10.

6. Cassens, Debra: "Expanded damages in elder abuse cases." *American Bar Association Journal*, January 1998, p. 39.

7. Gjertsen, Lee Ann: "Program resolves nursing home crimes." *National Underwriter*, December 15, 1997, p. 17.

8. James, Sallie: "Guardian pockets mother's money." *Sun-Sentinel*, March 21, 1998, p. 3B.

Chapter 4: The Risk of Needing Long-Term Care

1. Williams, Michelle: "Spock's wife pleads for help." *Sun-Sentinel*, February 28, 1998, p. 3A.

2. DeRosa, Robin: "Studying death." *U.S.A.Today*, February 26, 1998, p. 1D.

3. National Association of Insurance Commissioners: "NAIC Shopper's Guide" [Draft]. NAIC, August 7, 1998.

4. Quinn, Jane Bryant: "Who needs old-age insurance?" *Good Housekeeping*, July 1998, p. 74.

5. Love, Alice Ann: "Nursing home bill criticized." *Sun-Sentinel*, March 6, 1999, page 3A.

6. Littell, Bob: "LTC can be dream come true or nightmare." *National Underwriter*, April 20, 1998, p. 22.

7. Rimer, Sara: "Reaching 100 —not what it used to be." *Sun-Sentinel*, June 22, 1998, p. 3A.

8. McDonough, Edward: "Point of law: Medicaid penalty for lawyers." *The Salt Lake Tribune*, July 27, 1997. Online. Available: *http://www.sltrib.com/97/jul/072797/COMMENTA/28880.htm.* February 11, 1999.

9. Cassens, Debra: "Court enjoins law barring asset advice." *American Bar Association Journal*, July 1998, p. 36.

10. Gibson, William E.: "Nursing home bill halts Medicaid evictions." *Sun-Sentinel*, March 17, 1999, p. 3A.

11. Panko, Ray: "The power of suggestion." *Best's Review*, March 1999, pp. 75-79.

12. Koco, Linda: "LTCs for the late '90s hit the streets." *National Underwriter*, August 3, 1998, p. 25, 28-29.

Chapter 5: Is Long-Term Care Insurance Right for Me?

1. Jones, Chuck and Kim Perikles: "*LAN*'s 12th annual long-term care insurance survey." *Life Association News*, October 1998, pp. 70-85.

2. Wane, John and Lenny Anderson: "Long-term care offers p-c agents cross-selling option." *National Underwriter*, April 13, 1998, p. 2.

3. National Policy and Resource Center on Women and Aging: "A big decision for women: should I buy long-term care insurance?" *Women and Aging Letter.* Vol 1, No. 6, 1997. Online. Available: *http://www.aoa.dhhs.gov/elderpage/walltc.html.* February 26, 1999.

Chapter 6: Triggers and Taxes

1. Kelley, Lane: "Heat stroke victim once was homeless." *Sun-Sentinel*, June 27, 1998, p. 4B.

Chapter 7: Evaluating a Policy

1. Jones, Chuck and Kim Perikles: "Long-term care contracts are now tax qualified" [11th Annual *LAN* Survey of Long-Term Care Insurance]. *Life Association News*, November 1997, pp. 74-78.

2. Jones, Chuck and Kim Perikles: "*LAN*'s 12th annual long-term care insurance survey." *Life Association News*, October 1998, pp. 70-85.

3. "How will you pay for your old age?" *Consumer Reports* [Special Report on Long-Term Care Insurance]. October 1997, pp. 35-50.

4. Littell, Bob: "How insurers can avoid an LTC apocalypse." *National Underwriter*, April 27, 1998, pp. 82, 84-85.

5. Foley, Thomas: "Let's put the 'insurance' back into health insurance." *National Underwriter*, June 8, 1998, p. 7.

6. Health Insurance Association of America: "1996 long-term care insurance: premiums drop, sales soar" [HIAA Press release]. Online. Available: *http://www.hiaa.org/newsroom/press-releases/ release2.html*. October 13, 1998.

Chapter 8: Bells and Whistles

1. "Avoid the seven pitfalls of long term care insurance." Online. Available: *http://www.insure.com/health/ltc/pitfalls.html*. March 29, 1999.

Chapter 11: The Fine Print

1. Pass, Ted and Beverly Brenner: "LTC survey pinpoints underwriting issues." *National Underwriter*, November 16, 1998, pp. 7, 24.

Chapter 12: Group Long-Term Care Insurance

1. Davidson, Ronda Templeton: "The sandwich generation: finding a long-term solution to a long-term problem." *USAA Magazine*, November-December 1998, pp. 26-28.

2. Jones, Chuck and Kim Perikles: "*LAN*'s 12th annual long-term care insurance survey." *Life Association News*, October 1998, pp. 70-85.

3. Stanger, Janice: "Employer-sponsored long-term care insurance: a benefit for employees of all ages." Online. Available: *http://www.mr-longtermcare.com/ltc/experts/experts039.html*. April 2, 1999.

Chapter 13: Coverage for Home Health Care

1. Landers, Ann: [Column]. *Sun-Sentinel*, May 30, 1998, p. 2D.

2. Davidson, Ronda Templeton: "The sandwich generation: finding a long-term solution to a long-term problem." *USAA Magazine*, November-December 1998, pp. 26-28.

3. Singer, Stacey: "Elderly exploited by home caregivers." *Sun-Sentinel*, July 6, 1998, pp. 1A, 14A.

4. Van Buren, Abigail: "Caregiver's who take" ["Dear Abby" Column]. *Sun-Sentinel*, July 17, 1998, p. 2E.

5. Health Insurance Association of America: "Guide to long-term healthcare." Online. Available: *http://www.hiaa.org/consumerinfo/ guideltc.html.* March 24, 1999.

6. Kaplan, Samel X: "Community care benefits will attract seniors." *National Underwriter*, August 10, 1998, pp. 18-19.

Chapter 14: Alternatives to Long-Term Care Policies

1. Asinof, Lynn: "A second life: survivors of illness may find finances in need of care." *The Wall Street Journal*, April 23, 1998, pp. C1, C22.

2. Page, Wm. Scott: "Professionals in viatical industry welcome clear rules." *Sun-Sentinel*, March 29, 1999, p. 2B.

3. "Do you need insurance?" *Consumer Reports*, October 1997, p. 39.

Chapter 16: Where to Go for Help

1. "Family leave: it's a bumpy ride." *Sun-Sentinel*, August 12, 1998, p. 3F.

Chapter 17: Cloosing the Loop

1. Landers, Ann: [Column]. *Pittsburgh Post-Gazette.* May 10, 1998, p. H43.

INDEX

ABOUT THE AUTHOR

*L**es Abromovitz is a lawyer and member of the American Bar Associa-*tion. He has worked in the insurance industry for over fifteen years and arbitrated insurance disputes. As former Regional Insurance Manager for the Pennsylvania Insurance Department, Mr. Abromovitz counseled consumers on long-term care insurance issues and investigated agents for fraud and misrepresentation. He has authored and co-authored several books on insurance and insurance industry ethics. In addition, Mr. Abromovitz has edited several insurance books and written about this subject for Insure.com (the Insurance News Network) and many national magazines. He is author of the new book, *You Can Retire While You're Still Young Enough to Enjoy It: Straightforward Strategies to Get You There* (Dearborn Financial Publishing Inc., 1999). He and his wife, Hedy, split their time between Pittsburgh, Pennsylvania and Boca Raton, Florida.